WARFARE IN ENGLAND

WARFARE IN ENGLAND

BY

HILAIRE BELLOC

CAVALIER BOOKS
MILWAUKEE, WISCONSIN

Original copyright 1912 by Hilaire Belloc.
First published by Thornton Butterworth Limited, London, 1912.
Republished by Cavalier Books, Milwaukee, 2018.
Cover: *Sanctuary* by Richard Burchett, 1867.

ISBN: 978-1-948231-03-9

This edition © 2018 by Cavalier Books, Milwaukee, Wisconsin. All rights reserved. With the exception of short excerpts for critical reviews, no part of this book may be reproduced or transmitted in any form or by any means whatsoever without permission in writing from the publisher.

CONTENTS

I   THE STRATEGICAL TOPOGRAPHY OF ENGLAND.................9

II   THE ROMAN CONQUEST 30

III   THE NORMAN CONQUEST 51

IV   MEDIEVAL WARFARE—I 65

V   MEDIEVAL WARFARE—II..........78

VI   MEDIEVAL WARFARE—III 93

VII   THE CIVIL WARS 115

VIII   THE SCOTCH WARS 136

NOTE ON BOOKS 143

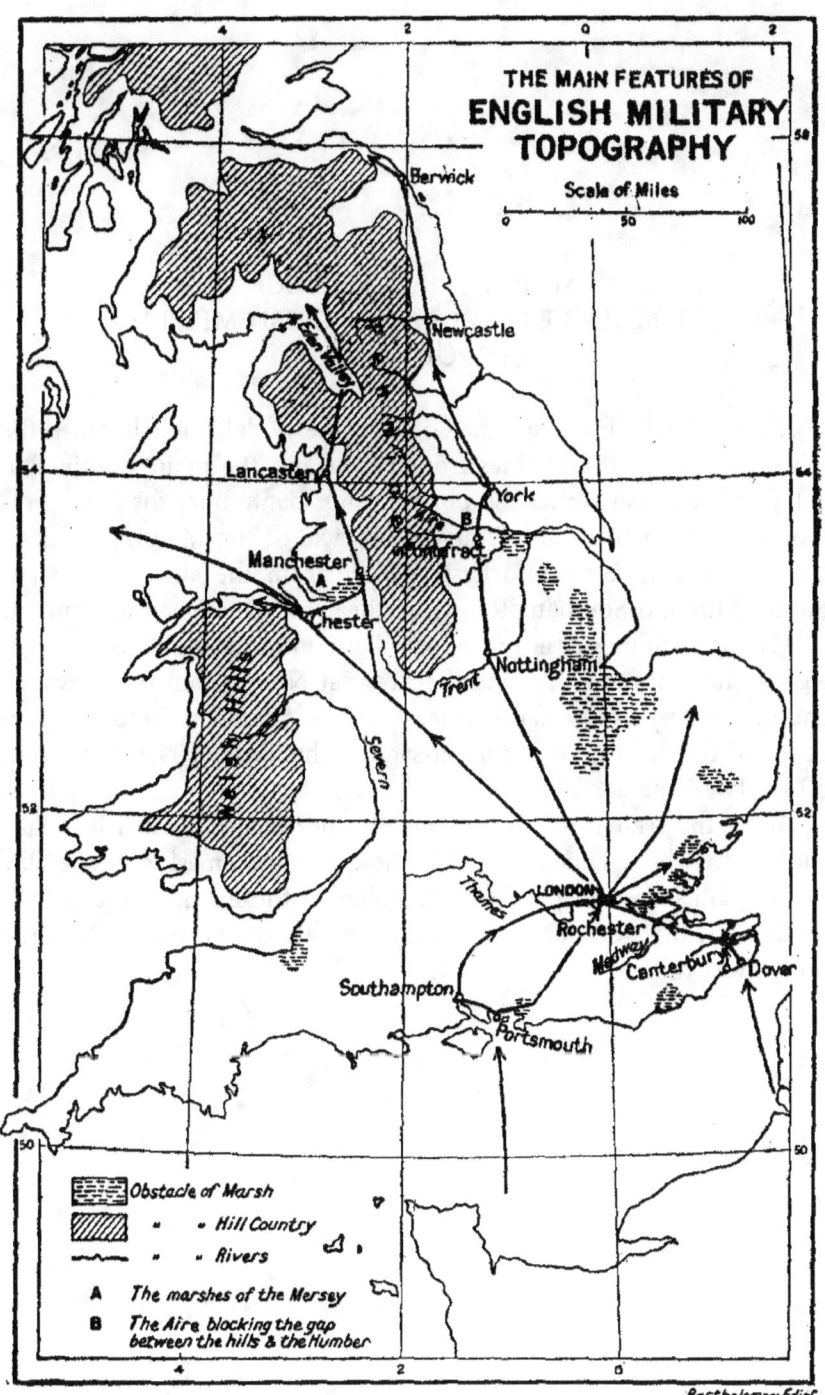

Frontispiece]   MAP 1 (see over)

MAP 1.—FRONTISPIECE
THE MAIN FEATURES OF ENGLISH MILITARY TOPOGRAPHY

Natural lines of advance to London: the nodal point because the lowest bridge on the Thames from Dover and the main Continental entry with alternative Kentish ports, having Canterbury for their common depot: whence the line at the obstacle of the Medway suggests the strategical point of Rochester, while from the alternative entry, Portsmouth and Southampton, two other roads may lead to London.

Also natural lines of advance from London to the North by the way *east* of the Pennines, crossing the Trent at Nottingham (or Newark), and the Aire by two passages which Pontefract defends. So to the main depot of the North, York, the passage of the Tyne at Newcastle, and of the Tweed at Berwick.

Or by the *west* through the gap of Stockport, defended by Manchester, to where Lancaster holds the gap between Morecambe Bay and the Hills over Shap Fell to the Valley of the Eden; with a branch to Chester, the port for Ireland and the gate of the road round the north-west hills.

CHAPTER I
THE STRATEGICAL TOPOGRAPHY OF ENGLAND

The military history of any country is largely determined by its *Topography*, that is, by the nature of its soil: where run its ranges of hills: how high, steep, or barren these may be: the situation of its better lands, with their chief towns: the position, depth and rapidity of its rivers, etc., etc.

The importance of such features lies in this: that by such features are aided or impeded the march of armies.

Of two armies organised each to destroy the fighting power of the other (whether by *breaking its cohesion*, by *cutting off its supplies*, or in any other fashion), *one* at least must be led to meet the other, and in nearly all historical cases *both* are led out to meet each other. Now, the "leading" of an army, the arrangement of its progress, differs in many material points from other kinds of travel: it has difficulties peculiar to itself, and must consult special conditions of its own. It has, therefore, received the special name of *Strategy*, which is simply the Greek for "leading an army."

An army, being a great body of men gathered together on one spot in far larger numbers than that spot would naturally support, must artificially arrange, as a rule, for a supply of *food*. Even if it be small, so that some densely populated country through which it is marching can support it, it will need supplies of *missile weapons* (if it uses these), of vehicles for its baggage, of horses to replace those lost, etc. For the continuous security of such supplies it will need *depots*, and these are naturally best provided by the opportunities which great towns afford.

Again, armies depend for their comparative efficiency very largely upon *speed*. Other things being equal, the army that can march fastest will beat the army that marches less fast. It can walk round its slower opponent; intercept him; appear unexpectedly on his flank; evade him when necessary, etc., etc. Moreover, this factor of *speed* is complicated in the march of armies by the necessity for arrangement, or *organisation*, without which a large body of men could not be moved at all, and which increases very rapidly in complexity with the size of the force one has to handle.

Two effects follow from this all-importance of speed, coupled with the peculiar difficulties attaching to the complex arrangements of an army.

These two effects are often not grasped by readers of history, because civilian history neglects military conditions: yet, until we grasp them, we cannot grasp the meaning of those campaigns by which history is decided.

They are, *first*, the necessity for *communications*; and *secondly*, the determining factor of *obstacles*.

When we read that "armies are tied to roads" the expression may puzzle us. *We* are not "tied" to a road when we travel. It is a convenience but not a necessity. A man will often for his pleasure travel for days in wild country without roads and make excellent progress. An army could conceivably advance without roads, though it would have to be a very ill-provided army, but it would advance very slowly and in great confusion even so. With stores, vehicles, etc., a road is necessary, and, what is more, speed is so essential a matter to military success that of two opposing forces that which commands the better roads has an advantage equivalent to a great advantage in actual numbers.

Again, to hold the junction of two or more main roads, or what is called "*a nodal point*," is of great advantage to one of two opponents, and it is an advantage which increases with the number of roads converging on that point. It gives him a choice of several lines of advance or retreat, and it permits him to watch, meet or intercept his enemy upon any one of them. The Bridge of London, with its converging roads from south-west and south-east, from north-west, north and east, is an example of this.

The converse to this necessity for *communications* is the determining effect of *obstacles*. Here, again, the reader of history is often puzzled by the importance military writers attach to an obstacle which, in civilian life, may be quite insignificant. A river a few yards wide, a range of hills nowhere precipitous may determine the fate of a campaign, though they would not appreciably delay a traveller. Why is this?

It is because of two things: first, because of that complexity of organisation which I spoke of above as necessary to armies; secondly because of the fact that armies are or may be *opposed* in their passage of any obstacle.

As to the first: if I come, during a walk across country, to a little river (such as the upper Avon, at Rugby), I make nothing of it. I am sure to find a bridge—and even lacking that I can fetch up and down for a convenient shallow, or get hold of a boat, or at the worst swim it. But 20,000 men cannot act in this way. Even if they have command of a bridge, they will have to crowd across it very few at a time. If they have no bridge, but must find a ford, they are still further delayed. If the bridge is cut or the ford deepened they must build a new passage. Even that little stream may mean the loss of a day—and the loss of a day may determine the war.

As to the second: the fact that an army advances in the presence of another army that desires to prevent its advance gives quite another meaning to *obstacles*, in the strategical sense of that word, from the meaning it bears in ordinary travel.

For instance: the Argonne hills in France are only 300 feet high and they are not steep. But they are of clay and densely wooded. Four roads cross them, and, at the beginning of the Revolutionary wars, these roads were held by the French with the Prussians marching against them. The Prussians forced one of those road-passages with some loss and after heavy effort. Another and most important one they failed to force, and their failure largely contributed to the French success that followed. On visiting the place one might wonder why the Prussians did not neglect the roads and go through the woods between, as a party of tourists might do to-day with no appreciable loss of time. The answer is that, had they done anything so foolish, their guns, their columns of marching men, their wagons with supplies of food, etc., would have melted after the first hour into a confused mob of halted, or, at the best, slowly advancing thousands, which the French from the roads on either side could have marched round and cut off at will.

It is so with every type of obstacle. What is nothing to a small body of men advancing in ordinary travel may be everything to a large body of men advancing against opposition.

It remains to mention one special form of obstacle which holds the first place in all the military history of civilised peoples. That form of obstacle is *Fortification*.

Fortification may be defined as an artificial obstacle raised intentionally by man, with the object of inflicting the maximum delay upon the attack at a minimum expense of men on the part of the defence.

Fortification is not primarily intended to keep an enemy permanently out of the particular area fortified. It is primarily intended to gain time, that is, to impose delay upon our enemy, and at the same time to increase the relative value of our own forces beyond their mere numerical value. One man behind works can prevent three men from going forward past those works.

Fortification is also intended to subserve three other military needs.

(1) It safeguards *depots* of supplies.

Thus fortified posts along a line of communications at sufficiently close intervals of (say) a day's march assure the permanency of supplies along that line and the security of their stores from sudden attack.

(2) It threatens the enemy's communications.

Thus we say that Belfort "blocks" the passage between the Jura and Vosges mountains, although that passage is twenty-five miles wide. We are certain that no army would be so foolish as to pass on either side, because, when it had passed, the garrison of Belfort would come out and "cut its communications," that is, prevent supplies from passing up to the front whither that army had proceeded. To stop that stream would be, of course, to destroy the army.

(3) It affords a sanctuary—when it is upon a sufficiently large scale, and well provisioned—for an army pressed by superior numbers in the field.

E.g. A Blue army, K, 60,000 strong is marching from Portsmouth against a Red army. A, only 40,000 strong at Alton, not thirty miles away—two days' march. Another Red army, B, also 40,000 strong, is coming up from Dorsetshire—four days' march away—to join army A. When A and B join, the Reds will have 80,000 against the Blue's

60,000. But if A gets caught before B comes up, A will be outnumbered and crushed. Then the Blues can turn on B and deal with him in his turn. Without fortification this is bound to happen, for the Blue army can strike between A and B. But suppose Winchester is fortified, A throws himself into Winchester and the Blues are checked. They cannot, with only 60,000 men, besiege Winchester (with 40,000 inside) *and* at the same time stand the attack of 40,000 more coming up behind them.

These four characters, then, attach to fortification. First and chief, the imposing of delay upon the enemy; next, the safeguarding of depots of supplies; then the threatening of an enemy's advance (so that, if it be properly garrisoned, he *cannot* neglect a fortified place); lastly, the affording of a refuge to an army expecting succour but not yet strong enough to meet the enemy in the field.

Warfare in England is not concerned with modern fortification, for there has been no fighting within the country since modern fortification was developed. But two forms of fortification we shall find determining the whole story of English warfare in the Middle Ages. First, the *walled town*; secondly, the highly fortified special point or *castle*. Each of these types acts continually as a delay in *time*, a guarded depot of *supplies*, a block to *advance* and a *refuge*, and each is found determining the results of campaigns from the eleventh to the sixteenth centuries.

These preliminaries being laid down, we can approach the main lines of English topography as illustrating English warfare. I will begin with the natural features, and conclude with the chief fortified points.

A plan of these two combined is the framework within which the whole story of warfare in England is acted.

Five great types of obstacle are found on the surface of the earth: hills, forest, marsh, river, and desert. The last is absent from England; the remaining four we will examine in their order.

As to hills—

Look at some good map of the whole island of Britain, in which mountain is distinguished from plain, and pasture and arable land from heath and waste.

The first thing that you discover is that the island is not divided into isolated stretches of arable and pasture land, each suitable for habitation, and each divided one from its neighbour by some belt of high or waste territory. The high and waste territories lie in great masses to the north and west, while the south and east form in the main, one habitable, arable, fertile district, cut by no such obstacles.

To this general scheme there are but two exceptions. One is the interference of an irregular mass of waste highland which cuts off the Scottish Lowlands from the North English plains, and, projecting in a tongue, divides these last into the Lancashire and the Yorkshire flats; the other is the isolated valley of the Eden.

As a consequence of this formation we shall find that the strategical topography of England was never concerned with that form of obstacle which most generally decides the strategy of warring or united kingdoms; to wit, the interference of high, waste, and barren land between two habitable bases, from one of which armies set forth, and to the other of which, as an objective, their advances are directed. So it was with Italy to the west and east of the Apennines; with the Lombard plain and the Germanies; with Provence and the crown of Paris. It has not been so with England. For the most part the armies that have marched to and fro over the territory of Britain have not had to concern themselves with the obstacle of difficult hill country, save in the case of the Pennines separating the Lancashire and Yorkshire plains, and even there no great action has depended upon any attempt to block an advance across them.

So much for hills; there remain forest, marsh, and river.

All these three are present abundantly upon the map of Britain. Forests have somewhat diminished in the course of centuries (though to nothing like the extent which is sometimes imagined); marsh has been temporarily drained and artificially masked by a system of hard roads and embankments, but it still would dominate the conditions of any—even a modern—campaign, east of the Great North Road, and would reappear everywhere else in its original extent but a very few years after a decline in our complex methods of dealing with it.

As to our rivers, they remain, for the most part, what they were; and by studying their conditions to-day we can determine their effect upon strategy in the past.

Now, of these three kinds of obstacle, *forest* has had least to do with our military history, *marsh* has proved the most formidable in character on particular occasions, *rivers* the most determinant of results in actual warfare.

A very large area of marsh intervening between two inhabited and cultivable areas would form an obstacle more serious than any other to an army, and one especially grave if it were extended in length, forming a natural barrier against communication between the two districts upon either side.

It so happens that a formation of this kind is very rare. And in the particular case of Britain there is but one district, and that a local and particular example, in which marsh has thus acted as a definite barrier to advance from a base to an objective. That case is the case of the marshes which cut off the Lancashire from the Cheshire plains.

Between Lancashire and the south, stretching from the Pennines to the sea, and leaving but a narrow gate by Stockport, a natural belt of marsh along the valley of the Mersey engaged in the past the military engineers of Rome, shaped the strategical plans of Prince Rupert in the civil wars, and has occupied in overcoming it the civil engineers of our own day.

This belt forms a true barrier, and one of the most clearly defined units in the strategical topography of England. It bars the whole advance to the north-west. It has made of *Manchester* (which commands the gap) a strategical point of the first importance for 1500 years, from the Romans to the abortive attack of 1644.

Elsewhere in England, marsh lies either in great areas apart from the main lines of military advance, or in isolated patches (as on the lower Parrett, in hollows of the Midlands such as Otmoor, etc.), which do not interrupt communication between one district and another. The main advance from the south to the north skirts and is not impeded by the fen land. The groups of marsh upon the south coast have isolated Sussex to the east and to the west, but have not affected military history because they could easily be passed to the north; while the only other considerable group, that cutting off Somerset from Devon, is turned with equal facility by the south.

Marsh land has often afforded a refuge for a broken force, as for the last of the resistance to the Norman Conquest; it has acted this part of a final stronghold upon three or four famous occasions in English history, but, save in the example of the Mersey valley cutting off Lancashire from the south, it has determined no part of the strategical history of Britain.

Of forest, there is even less to say; not even in early times was it either so dense or of such an extent as seriously to affect the march of armies. Forest has served the purpose of a refuge, and sometimes of a screen, but you do not find in the history of Britain, as you find in the history of Gaul, great stretches of dense woodland, the gaps or passes through which are gates to which a force is necessarily conducted and the defence of which may determine a campaign. The scale upon which Britain is built, the dispersion of its woodlands, their sporadic character and comparatively small extent in all periods, account for this negative feature in the history of British strategy. The armies of the French Revolution were all but lost by the forcing of the Argonne. Jemappes and Malplaquet each turn upon two neighbouring breaches in the woodlands of the Belgian frontier; the shepherding of the Duke of Cumberland on to Fontenoy was made possible by the presence of great and difficult tracts of trees; while to-day the Ardennes largely determine the calculations of the French and German staffs. Nothing of this kind can be predicated of warfare in England, and though, as we shall see later, wood necessarily enters largely into the details of a campaign and is, of course, as important *tactically* here as in any other country, it does not form, as it does so often abroad, a great topographical feature, nor canalise the history of war.*

It is upon the *river* system of Britain (in which I include, of course, the great estuaries) that the student of warfare in this island must particularly concentrate. It is the rivers and the profound funnels of sea-ways at their mouths which principally affect the march of armies in English history, and one might almost say that a study of strategy in Britain was a study in the hydrographical scheme of the island.

Before going further, it is as well to remark at once the following

---

* The reader must here be warned against an error childishly simple and yet perpetually repeated in the textbooks of English history. The word "forest" used in translating the Low Latin *foresta* does not mean forest in the sense of *woodland*. It means no more than waste lands under the special administration of the Crown. Thus the New Forest, the Forest of Elmet, and a dozen others that might be named, were never a real obstacle to any army, for no dense woodland occupied them, and their barren, ill-populated area was not too wide to be crossed in one day's march. Most of our historians have neglected this point and have confused themselves and their readers by so neglecting it. Thus Freeman talks with characteristic stupidity of the "pathless forest of the Andred's Weald," although but a few pages before he has been following the march of a great army right through it at the pace of thirty-three miles a day. The Andred's Weald (in Sussex) was a forest in the sense that it was waste land, being of stiff clay and badly watered, but it was never densely wooded and must always have been what we see it to-day, a collection of spinneys and heaths.

singular and capital complication presented by this type of obstacle. A river is a barrier to advance; it is a check, the possession of passages over which confers decisive advantage upon the possessor. A river thus acts as a determinant of strategy from within a very few miles of its source. The least stream, especially if it have low-lying and swampy banks, is a formidable hold-up to an advancing force, introducing to that one of two opponents who does not possess the artificial means of crossing it a fundamental disadvantage to be measured in hours of delay or in confusion of supply, or in unserviceable formation, any one of which, or all three together may involve him in defeat.

But a river is also, during a great part of its course, an avenue of advance and a means of communication as well as an obstacle. This is especially true of periods of low civilisation when roads are not thoroughly developed. What proportion of the whole length of the river will thus be available as a line of communications will depend upon the nature of the stream, upon the kind of boats available, upon the character of supply, of missiles, etc. But a certain large proportion of any considerable river will always be as much an avenue of advance along its course as a barrier to an advance transverse to that course; and this complication must be borne in mind when we consider the effect of a scheme of its water-ways upon the military history of any country.

Taking, then, the fundamental factor of strategy in this country to be the scheme of its rivers, let us see what that scheme is. The island of Britain stands in a tidal sea, the ebb and flow of which is greatly intensified by the formation of the coasts.

The great estuaries are so many funnels into which the flood pours with an especial violence, and, as a consequence, every part of the coast of Britain is provided with great natural highways into the interior, which highways "move along of themselves," aiding passage to and fro for a considerable distance from the sea coast.

No other European island is thus penetrated by the influence of the sea. Iceland has no such rivers, nor Sicily, nor Crete.

No continental region is under similar conditions (though Northern France and Belgium afford the closest parallel to them). And those conditions have moulded something like one-half of the story of warfare in this country. For the penetration of the island by its tidal water-ways is the determining element in the pirate invasions it has suffered from the east.

Again, apart from the tide, the country is penetrated to its very heart by a widespread river system which, with the exception of the Welsh mountains and that Pennine group to which I have already alluded, covers the whole country with a network of easy water communication. The considerable rainfall, its continuous character, the absence of any considerable heights to the south and east of the Pennines and of the Welsh hills, have made of Britain a land everywhere served and, under early conditions, everywhere vulnerable through water carriage.

Britain has three main categories of entry by water and of obstacles presented by water to the advance of an army.

These three main categories are—
(1) The great estuaries.
(2) The larger rivers which lead into the heart of the country.
(3) The numerous small coastal streams.

The first category stands by itself, although some of the great estuaries are the mouths of the larger rivers, and all of them lead up to river communication inland. It stands by itself because the estuary is a permanent obstacle which armies hardly or never negotiate directly, but which they are almost always compelled to turn. The smaller rivers, which are the characteristic form of obstacle all round our coasts and also the characteristic form of entry, are usually fordable at no great distance from their mouths, though there are exceptions to this general rule with which I shall deal later.

It is the second category, that of the larger rivers, which we must particularly note in establishing the strategic conditions of the island.

The reader will see at a glance that these longer river systems penetrating the heart of the island are but three in number. There is the system of the Thames, the system of the Humber or Trent, and the system of the Severn.

Now of these three the Severn can be left out. From the character of its stream, of its mountainous origin, of the geological formations through which it flows, the Severn has not proved a formidable barrier in the history of British warfare. It has not been defended as a frontier, and though its group of fortresses, Worcester, Gloucester, Shrewsbury, Bristol, have affected all our civil wars, the manœuvring of opposing armies has never strictly depended upon its line save once—in the campaign of Evesham, 1265.

The reason of this is threefold. In the first place, the river is too rapid and too uncertain to be used largely for commerce in all the upper part of its course. In the second place, it is easily and naturally passable in very numerous places, apart from its bridges. In the third place, the principal efforts of armies would be directed to no objective in approaching which the Severn would form a boundary. The struggle between the tribal kinglets of the Welsh hills and the successive governments of England was less a struggle between two races or two civilisations than a struggle between the mountain and the plain. Did the Severn correspond to the boundary of the Welsh highlands it might, in spite of the easy passages across it, have formed something of a strategical obstacle in our history. But it is not such a boundary. Good, arable land, and highly populated districts lay between it and the mountains. Wherever such land is to be found (as along the south coast of the Principality) the culture and social system of Eastern Britain, under its various names of Roman, Norman, English, or what-not, are also to be discovered. And the contest (which has never been on large and regular lines, but always of a scattered sort) between the hills and the plains below them, has not had to concern itself with the line of the great western river. In so far as there is any strategical plan to be discovered in the confused border fighting of this region it concerns not the Severn Valley, but the "Marches" of Wales. Its pivots and bases are nowhere to be discovered upon the stream of the Severn, but rather upon the line of strongholds, Newport, Hereford, Leominster, Ludlow, Shrewsbury, Chester; and on that line Shrewsbury alone is on the Severn, and is only accidentally connected with that stream, which nowhere forms a strategical element in the military problems of the Welsh border.

The remaining two systems which we have particularly to consider and which, between them, determine the strategical history of Britain, are those of the Humber and of the Thames.

Of all the rivers falling into the Humber, two only have permanently played the part of a military obstacle in the strategical history of the country, and that after a fashion that would not appear at first sight. The first of these is the Aire, the second the Trent.

The Ouse, the Swale, the Tees, the Wharfe all presented obstacles, of course, to any march upon the north; but the *Aire* was the main barrier—and that for these two reasons: first, that York, the capital of the north, was always the objective of a march northward, and that, of three rivers standing before York, the Wharfe, the Aire, the Don, the passage of the *Aire* was decisive because it was, so to speak, "at arm's length" from York. The passage of the Don at Doncaster was too far away to be usefully defended, that of the Wharfe at Tadcaster too close at hand: to fight there was to fight desperately near the city. But the second reason was far more weighty. The Aire bridges the narrowest passage between the Pennines and the estuary of Humber: what is still more important, it bridges the narrowest gap between the Pennines and the marshes that line the estuary of the Humber; no army could pass east of Rawcliffe: it could only pass with difficulty west of Wakefield in the hills. The Aire, therefore, serves, far less perfectly, the same purpose on the eastern side of the Pennines that the Mersey marshes do on the western side. It cuts the road to the north at a narrow gate, not much over a day's march in width.*

The Roman road crossed at Castleford, towards the western or hill border of the gap: the alternative later road at Ferry Bridge some four miles down stream. Both crossings were commanded during the dark and middle ages by the fortified post of *Pontefract*, which thus played on the eastern side of the Pennines something like the strategical part played on the western side by Manchester.

As to the Trent. The Trent leads right through into the heart of the Midlands, cutting England from east to west, while it has been more of an avenue of approach for invaders from the North Sea than an obstacle to advance from south to north.

The reason of this lies in the course of the river. It curls round the southern base of the Pennines—*across which from the south to the north no one would ever have to march*. When it has left the base of those hills it affords a barrier to a northward march across the plains over just a limited distance, for it soon begins to turn northward.

The principal crossing-place on a march north, from London to York, is at *Nottingham*, and the possession of the castle of Nottingham we shall therefore find to be of the first importance to medieval armies.

Lower down, where the Fosse Way touched it, and where the Great North Road passed the river, *Newark* defended it—and Newark, once at least in English military history (in 1643–4), was a pivot-point in the strategy of a campaign. Below Newark the Trent loses strategical importance. It no longer blocks the way north and south, but only

---

* Rawcliffe to Wakefield is somewhat over twenty miles.

the passage between Lincolnshire and Yorkshire—never of paramount importance to an army. The crossing of the Roman road at Littleboro' has never merited so much as an earthwork.

Finally we have the line of the Thames. The strategical value of the Thames lies in these two points: that the Thames forms an obstacle from above Cricklade to the Nore, cutting South England right in two; that South England is naturally by far the richest part of the island, the seat of its government and culture, the neighbour of Europe.

How thoroughly the Thames cuts South England a man may try for himself in this fashion: Let him go from Bristol to Bunsley by train; climb Bunsley Hill and thence look down upon the estuary of the Severn; then let him turn his face eastward and walk through Tetbury to Cricklade—it is easily done in a day—a matter of twenty odd miles: then let him try to cross the Thames at Cricklade through the water.

The Thames cuts South England with a clear military obstacle from side to side, from its eastern side to within a day's walk of its western: and South England is the heart of England, the origin of English measures and letters and all.

To these two points a third might be added—which is that the Thames line includes *London*, of which I shall speak in a moment. The importance of London in the strategical topography of England cannot be exaggerated; but in connection with the line of the Thames London may properly be regarded as no more than the outcome of that preponderance of the south in our civilisation which is its principal note.

The line of the Thames has been throughout English history the great obstacle present for an army to negotiate whether from the north, as when the Danes forced it at Cricklade, or from the south, as when Julius Cæsar forced it (whether at Brentford or Cowey Stakes), or William the Conqueror at Wallingford.

Its main part was defended above London by four strongly fortified posts, Oxford, Wallingford, Reading, Windsor: to these, Roman works at Cricklade and Dorchester should be added—but the four I have mentioned controlled the line throughout all the warfare of which we have record for fifteen centuries. Of these Reading, in the bend southward, counted least, for it could be neglected by whoever held Wallingford. Wallingford was the main crossing from the west, and Windsor—a day's march from London and exceedingly strong—was, after the Conquest, the chief of the line as terminal, and as supporting the largest garrison, and as threatening the immediate approach to London. London, and the way it controls its own crossing, I will presently deal with. Below London armies could not without vast preparation and a guarantee against opposition cross the tidal river.

I have shown how, in English strategics the southward extension of the *Pennines* is the principal hill-obstacle; but, on the advance northward, the marshes of the Mersey, of which the key is Manchester, the line of the Aire, of which the key is Pontefract, are the two barriers: how the Trent is held at Newark and much more at Nottingham: how the Severn is no true line: how the Thames is the principal line across South England.

To this should be added the position of Newcastle and Corbridge as holding the passage of the Tyne, of Berwick controlling that of the Tweed. I might have added the crossings of the marshy river valleys, by defended causeways (the *Stamfords, Stanfords, Stratfords, Stretfords, Staffords, Strettons*, Stattons, etc., all over England), and the rôle of the ports. But I have no space for more than the outlines of my subject.

I must conclude by dealing with three last points—one of capital effect, the position and value of London, the other two the main towns and the entry from Europe.

London.

No one can read the story of warfare in this country without being struck by one outstanding mark of it which separates it at once from the corresponding story of warfare in other European lands. That mark is this: the chief town of the island is after an early date, that is from the eleventh century onwards, never besieged nor even entered against its will by a hostile army.

From noting an anomaly of such importance the student is led to consider the causes of it, and so discovers that London has, for certain reasons which I will now describe, not only occupied a special position in all the military history of England, but very largely determined the fate of every struggle fought out upon the soil of this island.

In the first place, London always had and continues to have a numerical position of an extraordinary kind. It accounts to-day for something like a sixth of the population. It has often in the past accounted for a similar proportion of the population of its day. It has never had less than one-tenth of England within its boundaries, so far as we can estimate the numbers of the past. This feature alone would give it in the story of English campaigning a position quite different from that occupied by Paris, let us say, in the north of France, or Lyons in the south.

London, one town, the political feeling in which would generally run clearly in one current, favouring or resisting an invasion, or taking this side or that in a civil struggle, was also for centuries the best recruiting ground in the kingdom. Whoever had London could always be certain of a raw army and a large one: in this respect London appears as a deciding factor in the struggle of the aristocracy against John, in the Barons' Wars, even in the Wars of the Roses, and with a special weight in the Civil Wars of the seventeenth century.

But this is only one aspect of the numerical effect of London.

That numerical aspect it was which prevented a siege. There was never in England a hostile force sufficiently great to contain so considerable a perimeter as was measured by the walls of London. The river was too broad to be blocked for long, and it could always furnish supplies. No force was ever raised, perhaps none could ever be raised, large enough, I do not say to contain London in the military sense, even to oppose successfully such a great body as London could raise within itself for offensive purposes if it were menaced. The king of England never held London as the king of France held Paris. The Tower was never to London what the Louvre was to Paris. Throughout the six centuries which intervened between the last Danish fighting and the civil wars, London acts as the necessary ally even of regular governments; it is often their successful opponent; it is never entirely their subject, still less the victim of their conquest.

Nor is it upon numbers alone that this peculiar privilege of London reposes.

The economic position of London is also something quite anomalous and peculiar to the English State.

London is said to-day to exercise between a third and a fourth of the economic power of demand exerciseable in modern England.

In the past this control was, of course, infinitely simpler and less extended, while the actual *proportion* of economic demand which London could exercise compared with the rest of the country was smaller than it is now; but it was always very large, and translated into military terms it meant this: that London was always a base of supply. It could furnish money and it could furnish provisions. The Barons marching from Bedford in the campaign of Magna Charta recruited after that long march in London; but for the forage and remounts there obtainable their effort would have failed. At the other end of the story, in the Civil Wars, London provisions and pays the armies of the Parliament.

So much, then, for the peculiar value of London in English military history on account of its size, numbers, and wealth.

But there is more than this. London is also—as I have said—the nodal point of all the communications which bind eastern England. It was the point where the roads from the Yorkshire Plain and from the South Midlands and from East Anglia cross the Thames and catch on to the roads which give access to the Channel ports—especially those ports which command the narrower section of the Channel and stand over against the great continental approaches to this country, and which, therefore, will always be the principal entry from the continent for supplies, alliance, intelligence, or any other form of aid.

London thus blocks, and can permit or can restrain, communication by land between the eastern half of the island—the main part of it at least—and the southern counties and the Continent.

Finally, London by its position effectively divides England, when there is warfare in England, into a western and an eastern half as effectively as though a wall divided them. This topographical function by which London divides England strategically into an eastern and a western portion is singularly helped by the course of the Thames. The Thames takes its great bend northward just beyond Windsor, a day's march along the Roman road from London to the bridge at Staines; London commands everything eastward of that northern bend. In other words, a force from London can get across the Thames at Staines and be blocking an advance across the Thames from the south while an attempt to turn is checked by the northerly bend of the river. It is not until you get to the defensible point of Reading between its two water obstacles of the Kennet and the Thames that you find the first convenient passage over the river which escapes from the military influence of London. All marching from north to south or south to north accomplished in the face of a hostile London has therefore had to make the great bend westward, at least as far as Reading, which marks off the military story of eastern from western England.

This rule worked, of course, subconsciously rather than consciously in the simple strategy of feudal warfare, and even in the subsequent and more developed strategy of the Civil Wars, but though it has not appeared in the fixed plan of any particular general, it has worked none the less; and in the campaigns of the Barons in the thirteenth century, as in those of the Parliament in the sixteenth, you find the dividing line which London establishes between east and west passing not through London itself, but well to the west of it. Bedford, for instance, Windsor and the Bridge of Staines, all Surrey and all Sussex, are on the London side of this line, and troops condemned by the military obstacle of London to rely upon the west are based beyond the line, Warwick, Oxford, Wallingford, Reading, Basingstoke and Newbury: you do not find them fighting great general actions nearer to the capital than that.

The Towns.

Of the strategical effect of the towns it is enough to point out how many owe their value to their being fortified *depots* rather than points of natural strategical importance.

Of the latter sort are most of the old ports, such as *Bristol* or *Portsmouth*, *Chester* or *Southampton* or *Hull*. So are certain points clearly strategic, such as *Manchester* and *Pontefract*, whose power to hold a passage has been seen above, to which might be added *Nottingham* guarding the Trent, *Stafford* (where the road going N.W. from the Watling Street passed the marshes of the Soar), *Stamford* and *Huntingdon* holding the passages of the Welland and the Ouse respectively, *Rochester* the crossing of the Medway by the great road to the Continent, *Lancaster* the narrow passage between the Pennine Hills and the Irish Sea.

But many other towns have no such claim, and yet prove of capital importance in the military history of England, and that because, having arisen for reasons other than military, they found, once they had risen, excellent bases of supply and centres of population which could feed and equip an army on the march.

Of this kind are *Derby, Warwick, Northampton, Hereford*, etc.; and, of cities founded before the Roman military scheme, or at any rate not demonstrably necessary to its strategic plan, *Gloucester, Worcester, Salisbury, Leicester, Winchester* and *York*.

These great places, and fifty others, once established, become necessarily *depots* for supply. They are fortified. Once fortified they become *obstacles* as well as *depots*; *refuges* as well as *obstacles*, and the whole scheme of warfare is bound to turn upon their position. We shall find them perpetually recurrent in the story of our wars. Each has its castle, its garrison, its walls, its stores, and power to aid a force.

The Entries.

Lastly, we have the gates into the country from abroad.

Of these by far the most important are the Straits of Dover.

Here *Dover* itself, formerly possessing an enclosed inlet of the sea, is the chief entry (with its castle defending it), but in Roman times the Lympne flats (then a harbour) and Richboro' (then an island in the strait of Thanet) provided alternative entries, and, perhaps, Reculvers. *Canterbury* is the common depot of the straits. Farther down channel Pevensey, and later Rye and Winchelsea, entered into the same scheme, and one may say that *the coast from Beachy Head to the North Foreland, with its key at Dover*, is the gate into England from Europe.

A second crossing is that from the mouth of the Seine to the land-locked waters behind the Isle of Wight. Here *Portsmouth* (and earlier *Portchester*) and *Southampton* (and earlier *Bitterne*) are the entries.

From the first of these entries, as from the second, roads immediately strike for London, and by invasion along these the south-east of the island was secured.

The other entries, with few exceptions, are accidents of the shores: harbours which are chosen for their shelter, but in no relation to the proximity of a neighbouring stronghold or to the scheme of internal communication. Here invaders or exiles land for the convenience of a port, but not as part of any fixed plan: of such are *Milford Haven*; the mouth of the Humber (the now-swallowed-up *Ravenspur* in earlier, *Hull* in later times), the ports of the Wash, such as *Boston* and *Lynn*, *Preston* upon the Ribble, *Lyme Regis* and *Weymouth*, *Shoreham* in Sussex, *Orford* in Suffolk or *Fowey* in Cornwall, against which Essex was pressed in the Civil Wars; with many others. All these are eccentric to the true strategics of the island, and are but a crowd of accidental entries into it from the outside. They are like the *windows* of a house of which the south coast entries between the Solent and the Thames are the *doors*.

Within this strategical framework of England, with its great ridge of the Pennines, its bar to northward advance by the Mersey and the Ribble on either side of these, its great obstacle, depot, and nodal point of London, its line of the Thames, its continental entry from the south and east, there is played out a business of war from the first century to the seventeenth.

I propose in this book to group that business as follows—

First—the Roman Conquest, to which, must be added a mention of the pirate invasions of the fifth and sixth centuries (we know scarcely anything of them), and some words on the struggle of the ninth century with the Pagans, though that rough-and-tumble, which nearly cost us our lives, had little analysable strategy about it.

Secondly—the Norman Conquest.

Thirdly—the Feudal Fighting of the Middle Ages, which I will divide into three chapters, the "Campaign of Magna Charta" in 1215-16, the "Barons' Wars" of 1264-5, and the "Wars of the Roses," 1452-1485.

Lastly—I will deal with the Civil Wars of the seventeenth century.

I will briefly add, by way of appendix to our domestic military history, the very simple strategics of the various expeditions into Scotland and Wales.

A few general considerations must be touched upon before we deal with these separate divisions of our subject.

The first is this: The larger lines of strategics within the island only appear when some universal effort is being made, as, for instance, when the Romans or the Normans are attempting their conquest, or when the whole land more or less is harried by savage incursions from the North Sea. Under such conditions the whole map of Britain is brought into play, and the great natural roads of access towards the objectives of either party, the great natural obstacles present in the use of such roads, are plainly apparent and mould the whole story. But in other interludes, when fighting was more promiscuous and its objects less general, the large strategical lines of the island either disappear or become exceedingly confused. Thus, in the petty warfare waged between the kinglets of the Dark Ages, it is impossible to establish any reasonable strategical plan. Again, in the anarchy of Stephen's reign, and the struggle between that King and the Empress Matilda, you get no clear lines by which the movements and effects of fighting bodies can be explained. On the other hand, the great Norman sweep from south to north, and even the major operations of the Barons' Wars in the thirteenth century, lend themselves to a true strategical plan.

Secondly—the Island of Britain is remarkable for its immunity from organised invasion on the part of civilised armies.

Were it otherwise we should find the history of warfare in Britain perpetually following certain well-defined tracks, as does, for instance, the history of warfare in Northern Italy or in the Netherlands, both of which districts of Europe have throughout recorded history suffered repeated invasion by properly organised forces, always bound to enter through the same gates and to follow certain lines laid down by nature for the advance and retreat of great bodies of men.

Save for such rare episodes, English military history is taken up with domestic war.

Now, it is the characteristic of such warfare that the two parties to it do not proceed each from a distant base towards a distant objective. Cities are often divided against themselves, at least in the inception of such struggles. The strongholds which attach themselves to the one or to the other party will be scattered more or less at random throughout the whole kingdom. Therefore a Civil War—especially in its earlier stages—is strategically complex, and it is only towards the later part of it, when one side is definitely getting the upper hand and has subdued whole districts, that the main lines of strategy reappear.

Thirdly—it must be remarked that warfare upon any large scale has been unknown in England since the Reformation. If we include the Civil Wars, small as were the numbers engaged and slight as was the military effort they involved, we can yet say that England has not experienced warfare upon any scale worthy of historical record during the whole period in which modern arms have developed since (and during) the wars of Louis XIV.

All that great story of the professional armies of the eighteenth century leaves England without any strategical history, and one of the few great strategists of whom human annals bear record, the Duke of Marlborough, expanded the military story of his nation in fields that had nothing to do with the topography of his own land and with troops few of whom were English. The only military rôle he played in England itself was the exceedingly unpleasant part of a domestic traitor who would sell, as occasion served, his King, his country, or his sister.

This singular distaste which Englishmen have shown during the last three hundred years for an armed decision cuts out of the military history we are about to examine the whole development of modern artillery and of modern fortification. This last gap is in particular regrettable because it is of a special interest to the student of military things; the way in which earthworks arose to meet the new ballistic arm which, from the seventeenth century onwards, has decided sieges, the classical effect of Vauban; the whole story of defence between the Dutch Wars of Louis XIV and the capital modern example of Port Arthur; the perfection of the old enclosed star with its ditch, bastion, and hornwork, yielding gradually to the advance of artillery, and replaced by the modern Ring fortress. All this is absent from the history of British warfare. Those numerous towns scattered over the Continent, and especially thick in north-eastern France, where you may see still intact the great defences of that age of earthworks, have no parallel here (save in one exception, which is to be discovered in the works round the North Gate of Berwick), while the modern Ring fortress is utterly unknown; and even our great naval bases remain, for all purposes of attack by land, unprotected at the moment I write these words.*

---

* July 1912. It may interest the reader to know that Portsmouth, the only naval base of which a serious defence was ever attempted, and one singularly adapted for such defence, has now been definitely abandoned under a theory that the moment the Fleet ceases to be supreme at sea, a modern British Government would accept peace upon the enemy's terms.

CHAPTER II
THE ROMAN CONQUEST

In order to understand the strategics of Britain when it was part of the Roman Empire and during the Conquest which preceded its existence as a province, it is necessary to observe a certain number of fundamental points, some of common knowledge, others less often remarked.

(1) That the coming and going of military effort throughout that period radiated from a centre at Rome. In other words, the effort was an effort from South to North.

(2) Both to the genius of the Roman civilisation and to the military practice consequent upon that genius the sea was abhorrent: to occupy a province separated by the sea was for the Roman government an exceptional feat. The shortest sea passages take an exceptional prominence in the first four centuries of our era, and provinces separated by the sea—as Africa and Britain—are raided by barbarians (and ultimately lost) with greater ease than those which had a continuous communication by land.*

(3) The Roman Empire was a system based in the main upon agriculture. It made little effort to extend its rule over barren or mountainous tracts. That is why there was no determined effort to occupy the Baltic Plain and the more northern of the Germanies, the Marshes of Frisia, etc. That is why the Pyreneean tribes largely escaped from the Roman organisation. That is why Brittany, Wales, and the Highlands—though two of them fell within the boundaries of the Empire—retained, and partly retain to this day, their original speech and customs.

---

* Let it be noted that the "fault" between Greek and Latin, East and West, was the Adriatic.

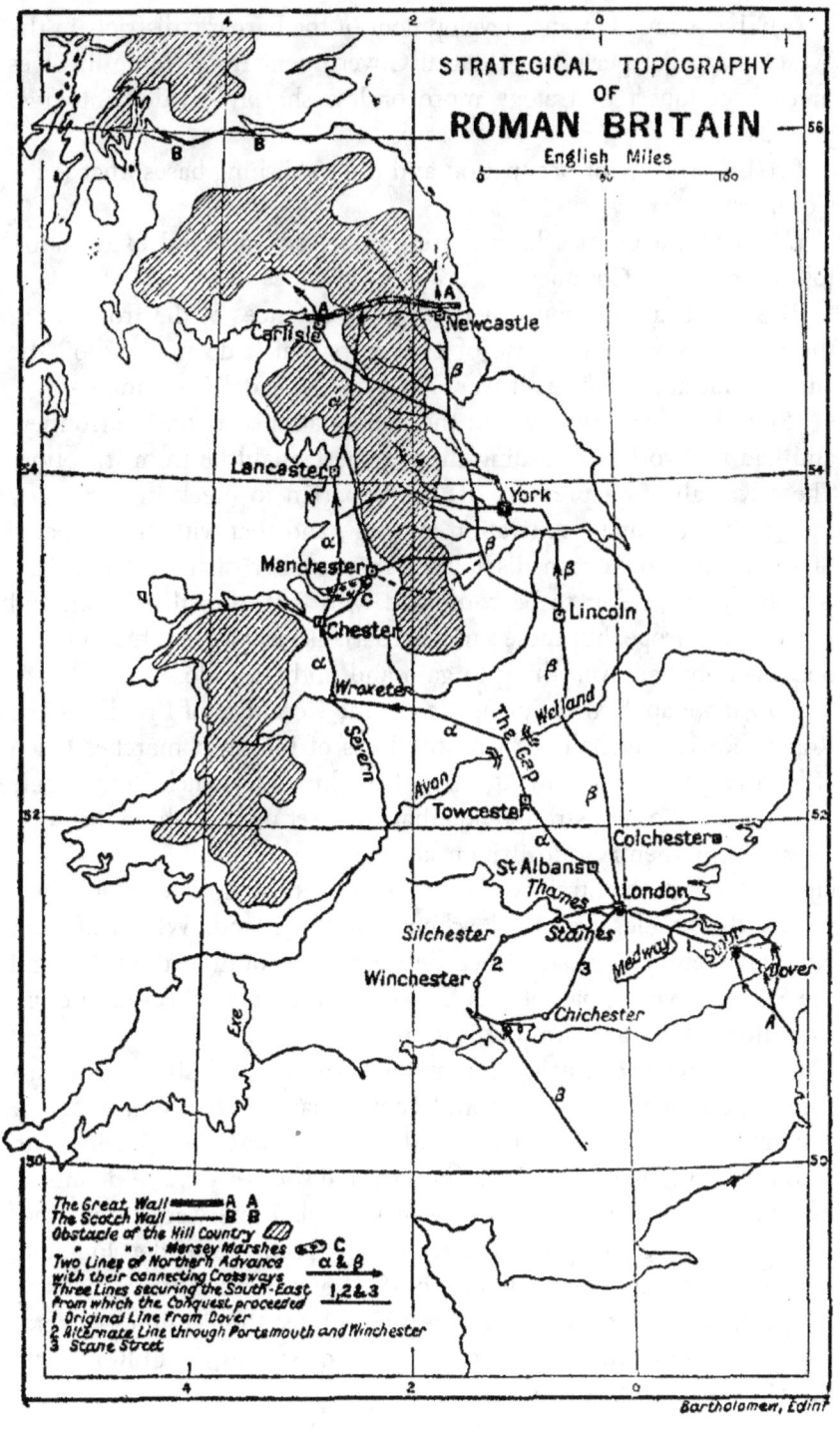

(4) The occupation and development of the barbaric districts in the West during the period of Central Government from Rome involves in each conquest a strategy more or less sharply divided into two periods.

(*a*) The strategy of occupation and of establishing bases: that is the Conquest.

(*b*) The strategy of a later more gradual advance and exploitation following on the Conquest.

This last is always concerned with the defences of the frontiers of the empire, save in the case of civil wars which do not despoil the citizens but are fought as it were "over their heads." Therefore—

(5) The Roman army was in the main stationed upon the frontiers and had the work of guarding them as best might be from irruption. There was always a pressure of the barbarian to break in and enjoy the results of Roman cultivation and law, and that without the pains of submitting to Roman discipline. The number of these barbarians was, of course, never to be compared with that of civilised mankind in western Europe, but these same barbarians were a perpetual menace because they had everything to gain and nothing to lose.

Now if we apply these principles to the Conquest of Britain by the Roman forces we shall see why the lines of the great marches (such at least as have come down to us), of the limits to which Roman rule extended, and of the strongholds that were set up, lay where they did.

The Roman entry into Britain lay at first entirely and always principally through the Straits of Dover, a gate whose unique value determined the whole strategical scheme of the island. When later an alternative entry was established between the mouth of the Seine and the Solent, it was apparently as far west as the Romans cared to carry their lines of regular communication.

From these two entries, but notably from the first, the Romans came upon all that southern and central part of Britain which may roughly be called "The Plain," and which it was their business to colonise, develop, and exploit. The extreme south-west, the peninsula of Devon and Cornwall, they long neglected. There were three other regions which could play no part in their scheme of development, which were exceptions or hindrances or boundaries to their civilising effort: these three regions were the Welsh hills, the Pennines (including the group of hills round the lakes and beyond the Solway), and the Highlands of Scotland.

The Welsh hills led nowhere. Their occupation was not worth the Roman while, but so long as irritating forays could be conducted from them down eastward on to the plains it was necessary to control or at least to check their inhabitants. But we should form a very erroneous opinion of those great four centuries of high civilisation from which modern Europe sprang, if we imagined the Roman mind to fall into what is called now-a-days the "Imperial spirit," or to waste effort upon what was not of material advantage to the commonwealth. There was no such object discoverable in the occupation of the Welsh mountains, nor did the Roman civilisation ever permeate the principality. Wales was, of course, affected, as was all western Europe, by the Roman idea, because that idea was coincident with civilisation itself. Wales afforded a sort of refuge into which the legends and even the traditions of civilised order, as it existed when the first pirates came to disturb it, might retire and survive. But Wales was not in the first four centuries what the English South and the Midlands were, or what Picardy or Normandy were. It might rather be compared to that land of the Basques in the Pyrenees at whose frontiers the Roman influence seems to cease which, with the exception of the great Roman road traversing it, is almost unaffected by the work of the old civilisation, and which, like Wales, has retained a tongue older than the advent of the Legions.

Of the Highlands, or Caledonia, the same is true, but in an even greater degree. For long there was an effort of the Roman arms against the Borders, as a region whence raids might perpetually be directed against the wealth and cultivation of the Lowlands. Agricola had some vast and unconcluded plan of conquest. It came to nothing. Four generations later Severus marched up against the same unexploitable and barren land, but there was no inclusion of its glens and mountains within the empire, although the attempt to protect from its clans the fields of the Lowlands determined much of the strategy of the island.

With the third hill-region, the Pennines, it was otherwise. This irregular mass of moor, furnishing no wealth to the conqueror save here and there metals, was not so situated that it could be neglected as Wales was, or left outside the Roman orbit as was Caledonia. The fertile plain of York, the arable land of Lancashire, were divided one from the other by the long tongue of the Pennines, and though there is reason to believe that the Lowlands of Scotland were but sparsely inhabited, yet it was a continual motive in Roman civilisation to occupy them because they formed a base for agricultural wealth. That irregular mass of hills, therefore, which includes the Cheviots, Galloway, the Lake District and the Pennines, was treated in a third and different fashion from that which the Romans used with Wales upon the one hand and Caledonia upon the other. The submission of tribes in Galloway was obtained but not enforced. The arable lands of the great Yorkshire plain and of the Lancastrian western belt were both permanently occupied and permanently developed; and since the tongue of the Pennines between these was a very serious obstacle to the communication of armies and of government, it was necessary to bridge it with roads permanently held by fortified posts. Those roads followed the lines which communication has since always used, much the same as those which the principal railways take to-day.

The principal line on which that obstacle of the Pennines was cut was the gap which may indifferently be called that of Ilkley or of Skipton. Through this the road which had its western base at Ribchester followed past Broughton to Ilkley and thence through Tadcaster to York.

This main passage of the Pennine obstacle permitting communication between forces to the west and to the east of it would have left each in peril at any considerable distance from its two termini. Northward from that gap to the Wall (which we shall see in a moment was the permanent limit of Roman power) was a distance of over eighty miles. Southward, to the last fastnesses of the Peak, the distance is very nearly as much. Either of these distances means four days' heavy marching, though a small body heavily pressed might attempt the matter in three.

Suppose, therefore, two forces making their way northward—the one by the Lancastrian, the other by the York plain—they would be operating in isolation one from the other when either was more then twenty miles to the north or to the south of Ribchester upon the west, or of Ilkley upon the east.

We shall see in a moment that advance by the east as from the west was a necessary part of the strategics of the island during the Roman occupation, and it was essential to cut the obstacle of the Pennines in more places than this one bridge of the Skipton Gap.

So far as we can judge by existing remains the obstacle was cut in at least two other places. It was cut from the Valley of the Tees to that of the Eden, over the high but workable gap now used by the railway between Bowes and Kirkby Stephen.* This communication between west and east bisected, as nearly as was practicable, the northern eighty miles. As for the southern, between the Ilkley Gap and the Peak, they appear to have been cut by a way that can be followed from Manchester to Slack, which thence proceeded down the valley of the Calder. This line does not exactly halve the southern part of the Pennine obstacle, but is at any rate a good day's march southward down from the Ilkley Gap; while over the Peak district itself there seem to have been several ways, two converging on Buxton and one (not so certainly Roman) passing half way between that town and the Manchester-Slack road, which I have already mentioned.

We saw in the last section that of the various sorts of obstacle which Britain presents the rivers would prove the most serious, and it is upon the rivers that the Roman conquest turns. They are the limits of each belt of occupation decided upon during the process of the conquest, and the strategical bridges over them determine the course of the Roman roads and the springing up of the Roman strongholds.

The main great obstacle in the south of England is, as we have postulated, the Thames. In Cæsar's abortive invasion (his second), as in the later conquest, the Thames is the determining factor of the first struggle. In Cæsar's second invasion his principal difficulty was to find a crossing of the Thames in order to get at his enemy, Cassivellaunus, whose territories lay north of London. Where Cæsar crossed has been the subject of innumerable pamphlets, papers, and even books. By far the greatest authority on the whole subject of this invasion, Dr. Rice Holmes, has determined it impossible to decide, but it would seem to be either at Cowey Stakes or at Brentford.

We are equally ignorant of the place where the Thames was passed when the conquest of the island was seriously attempted nearly a century later under Claudius, though the best inference points to a bridge at London.

At any rate the Thames is the great main obstacle upon which turns the strategy both of Cæsar's invasion and of the best part of the conquest.

But apart from the Thames two other rivers stand between the

---

* The line runs from Greta Bridge through Raycross to Brough, always a little northward of the modern railway, and more to the north of it after the high land is left.

entry into the country through the Straits of Dover and the approach to the Thames itself. These two are the Stour and the Medway. It was at the Stour that Caesar fought his first big action. It was at the Medway that Plautius, going before Claudius as his general, forced the first stand of the British, probably near Rochester. The first great Roman road of the conquest lies from Dover through Canterbury and Rochester to London.

When, later, the landlocked water of which Portsmouth is the modern, Porchester the ancient, entry was taken as an alternative terminus for crossing the Channel, another strategical route had to be devised for the negotiation of the Thames obstacle and the reaching of London, and this proceeded at first through Bitterne near Southampton, then through Winchester and Silchester, to Staines, where a permanent bridge was established, while, later, a second and shorter cut was made through Sussex for reasons I shall presently describe.

We see, then, that the first Roman strategical efforts were, in point of time, concerned with the negotiation of the rivers of the south and east; the Stour was crossed at Canterbury, the great marching road led across the Medway at Rochester to a bridge at London; a second and later approach ran from the great port on the Solent, crossed the Itchen at Bitterne, and, curving round by the west, struck the Thames at Staines, approaching London from that point by the north bank of the river.

To these two simple elements in the strategics of the south-eastern district, which was the base from which all the conquest of Britain proceeded, a third element should be added. The length of the detour from Portsmouth to London by way of Winchester and Staines was so considerable as to suggest during some period of the Roman occupation the building of an expensive but strategically valuable short cut by which in time of need troops could be hastened to what was soon the largest town in Britain and the main crossing of the Thames.

A military obstacle far less formidable, of course, than such a range as the Pennines or than any considerable river menaced an army trying to take the shortest cut from the south coast to London, and this was the clay land of the Sussex Weald. It would be error to imagine that there was either dense forest or a complete absence of culture and habitation in this belt, but without a carefully engineered road it would proceed for a breadth of over a day's march on two things which armies must avoid: bad water and bad going. Save after a spell of dry weather, it would be very difficult to get a considerable body of men across the innumerable ghylls and the deep clay of the Weald. A line as direct as physical circumstances would allow was therefore run from Chichester to London. Much of this military work has survived and, though bearing a different name in various parts, is generally known by the title of The Stane Street.

To this simple scheme of south-eastern Britain in the strategics of the Roman period there is nothing to add save that Canterbury was the depot for various landings round the Promontory of Kent, that a fortified post existed—perhaps for the purposes of watching pirate raids, or perhaps as a fort in connection with London—at Pevensey, and that though all vestiges but two have disappeared of its trajectory, a road ran from London to the nearest point upon the coast, the mouth of the Adur.

We may sum up, then, and say that the scheme of south-eastern England for Roman military purposes was an approach by two main roads from either of the two alternative entries into the country, each road crossing the Thames by its own bridge, and the western one shortened by a straighter line engineered at some unknown period during the occupation.

But, as I have said, this south-eastern region, let us say 200 miles by 100, though its possession gave an invader three of the principal towns, the main harbours, the wealthiest corn lands and all that he needed to proceed upon his task, was only a base from which the rest of the Conquest must proceed, and I will next show what extension that effort took, upon what lines, and what part the rivers play in delimiting it.

Four main phases established Roman rule in Britain after the south-east (with its two, and later, its three, great roads on London) was secured. These were—

(1) The occupation of the country up to a line determined by the Exe, the Lower Severn, and the line of two rivers, the Ouse and the Welland, which exactly cut off South-Eastern England, making one line from Tewkesbury to the Wash.

(2) The extension northwards of this first occupation into the Midlands; with the corresponding attempt upon the Welsh hills which almost ended in disaster and in an abandonment of the island on account of the great rebellion in the south and east.

(3) The long business with the Brigantes, that is with all that we

now call the North Country, and that business dominated by the obstacle of the Pennines.

(4) The temptation to exploit the Lowlands of Scotland with the insuperable difficulties in the face of a successful exploitation thereof, this imposing a lasting hesitation upon the limit which the Empire should here set to its administration, and involving the construction of the two walls.

When we have examined these four phases of the Roman Conquest, having no information worth the gathering of the strategics following upon the conquest, we shall have concluded this first section in the elements of British Strategical History, in which the rivers were the principal determinants, and enter its second phase, the Dark Ages, in which the rivers are again the determinants, no longer as obstacles, but as avenues of advance for the Pirates.

To fix a strategical frontier for the first period of the occupation might seem to a modern Englishman a difficult thing. We are so used to numerous made roads, to travel by railway, to bridged rivers, etc., that we have lost the "eye" for a military obstacle in modern England, and we see none definitely drawn upon the map, protecting the south and east from sea to sea.

Though we are not absolutely certain where that first strategical frontier was found, we can infer upon evidence which it would be too long to detail here, but which is sufficient for our conclusion, that it lay in a line drawn from the mouth of the Welland to the neighbourhood of Gloucester. On the west it was the line of the Exe. Roughly speaking, therefore, a triangle was enclosed and occupied, which triangle was the wealthiest and most populated, and most easily garrisoned and developable part of ancient Britain. Let us examine the nature of such a temporary frontier.

The Severn, to well above Gloucester, is an obstacle too formidable to need comment, but the Warwickshire Avon is also capable of defence under primitive conditions as far as the neighbourhood of Coventry, that is, well above the modern site of Warwick.*

---

* So true is this, that the Fosse Way bends to the right in order to avoid a passage of the river below the point I have named. It is pointing right at the town of Warwick until it reaches Moreton, when it bends off eastward. It does not attempt the Avon until right away up at Church Lawford, and having crossed it bends to the west again. The Warwickshire Avon is indeed only crossed in one place by an ancient road, and that is by the Buckle, but that is frankly an engineering feat, and its character

This line of the Avon was further strengthened by a considerable string of woods. It is always an error peculiarly facile and misleading to exaggerate the amount of woodland in ancient Britain compared with that of the present time, but it can be historically proved that in the case of the upper courses of the Warwickshire Avon a considerable forest, which was later as considerably reduced, existed.

If a man follows the Avon to its very first springs he is within half an hour's walk of the first springs of the Welland. It would be more accurate to say, perhaps, that the very highest waters of these brooks, where each river rises, almost touch, but at any rate a man leaving the Avon near Wellford Station, is on the Welland at Bosworth Hall within two miles of walking.

So high up in their courses neither stream affords a strategical obstacle, but the Welland does begin to have some such effect in the neighbourhood of Market Harborough. A few miles below, in the neighbourhood of Ashley, that effect is very pronounced, and land which was originally marshy land is clearly apparent. From that point uninterruptedly to the sea, the Welland forms a well-marked and highly defensible line. Thus to cross it at Stamford the great Roman road to the north had to pass by an engineered causeway which has given the town its name, while immediately below that point begin marshes which even in their modern shape have been hardly reclaimed from the sea, and into the creeks of which a high tide reached in Roman times. Roughly speaking, then, the gap or gate in this first strategical frontier of the Roman was, in its broadest acceptation, a matter of thirty miles, or a day's march, on either side of a central station, and where that central station stood we can fairly well fix, although the temporary work of the early occupation is naturally overlaid by later work.

Right through that gap runs the Watling Street, the great Roman line of communication from the south-east to the north-west. A garrison upon that line would command the gap. Towcester, though a good day's march to the south of the line itself, did so command the gap, for any considerable body attempting to pass it could be struck by a force at Towcester to the left or to the right as it did so.

---

in no way interferes with the truth that the Warwickshire Avon was a true strategic frontier, for the Buckle Street is carried across the low-lying and originally marshy land of Bidford by a causeway.

The reason that the Exe formed a natural boundary obstacle upon the west lies in the rugged nature of the country beyond that river in the Damnonian Peninsula. The great system of straight Roman roads does not penetrate beyond the Exe, and though it is true that the upper waters of that river are a mere brawling stream and no obstacle at all, it must be remembered that Exmoor, through which they run, is in itself a formidable and considerable obstacle. From at least Tiverton downwards to the sea, the Exe is a true boundary, and the gate between Tiverton and Exmoor, which we may make as narrow as we please, would be at its broadest quite easy to guard even if there were formidable forces menacing the Romans to the west of that line. But there were none.

In the first phase, then, of the occupation, you have the strategical frontier of the Welland, the Avon, and the Severn continued in the line of the Exe, and thus enclosing all that was most valuable and most populated in the province which Rome was attempting to annex.

The position and numbers of the forces used by the invader do not concern us in this study of strategic topography. But it is worth remarking that even so early Colchester, St. Albans, and London in the heart of the newly annexed district were organised as Roman towns.

The next phase consists in the further advance of the Romans into the Midlands, and the military peril which this rapid extension involved. The forward movement occupied some fourteen or fifteen years from, say, the year 45 or 46 to, say, the year 60 or 61 of our era. It was, perhaps, in 49 that a garrison was moved up to Lincoln on the one side, and probably to Wroxeter under the Wrekin on the other, and the object of all that forward movement was a task which invariably falls upon a conqueror, and is the most difficult of his problems; the coercion of districts which, while exterior to those it is worth his while to occupy, furnish reservoirs of discontent and of opposition: hill-places to which the defeated rulers of the fertile plain can retire, and fastnesses of little value to commercial development, but of indefinite military value as a reserve whence attack can proceed.

Two such general areas threatened the new Roman province.

First, the hill land of the Pennines, which with the fertile plain on either side and all that we now call the North Country, was held in the main by the confederation of the Brigantes.

Secondly, and at first more formidable, the hill land of Wales.

It was against this second outlying part that the Roman General Ostorius moved. The hill land of Wales was occupied in the north by the Ordovices, in the south by the Silures. The division between the two lies roughly where to-day lies the division between North and South Wales, namely, in that tongue of the lowland which advances into the heart of the country and reaches the base of Plinlimmon. It was against the first group, or Northern Welsh, that Ostorius advanced, and this because in so doing he could cut the forces that harassed him into two. He marched upon the mouth of the Dee, thus putting himself between the Pennines and the Welsh hills. He broke an attack from the Brigantes on his right, and at some unknown place upon his left, possibly as far south as Llanidloes, he defeated the independent tribe and that powerful King Caractacus, who had fled from the conquered territory, and had menaced the first Roman Border.

Successive generals continued an unceasing war against the tribesmen of the north and of the south in these mountains. The climax and actually the final success of that effort consisted in a march along the northern shore of the Principality, the crossing of the Menai straits, and the rout of the British in Anglesey. It was in the year 60 that this took place, and it was thought necessary to push so far because Anglesey was the centre of the national religion, and therefore of the national resistance, so far as it could be called national, which the Romans had to face. Under the conditions of so recent a conquest that distant march beyond the Welsh hills was an error. The country in the south-east rose, a very formidable rebellion destroyed the Roman population of the three new towns, St. Albans, Colchester, and London, and the rebellion under the leadership of Boadicea was within an ace of success.

If the battle which decided its fate had gone against Roman arms, it is fairly certain that no further attempt would have been made to reoccupy the province, and that Britain would have suffered the fate of the Baltic Plain or of Ireland, and have remained external to the body of ancient civilisation. As it was the Roman forces returning from the north-west under the leadership of Suetonius met and defeated in a defensive battle the very numerous forces with which Boadicea had advanced against it from her crushing of the Roman garrisons in the south and east. Where that action was fought we have no means of deciding. We know its tactical character from a fairly minute description. The trained Roman body far smaller than its opponents lay in occupation of a narrow gap between two woods.* The main British charge was broken, and after the massacre that followed South-Eastern Britain was finally and permanently held.

The third and fourth phases of strategic topography during the Roman occupation do not follow, but are contemporary; they consist in the long struggle with the Brigantes whose fastness was the Pennines, and the attempt to include the lowlands within the area which the Roman system of development and exploitation determined to control.

The struggle with the Brigantes and the varying success of the attempt to hold the lowlands of Scotland are each determined strategically by that formation of the northern hills to which attention has already been called in previous pages.

Rome in occupation of Lincoln and of the fertile plains to the west which are watered by the Idle, the Aire, and the Don, could not leave unconquered the great Plain of York, which was as much a matter for her energies as any of the corn lands of the south.

But if she occupied that plain she must defend it against incursions from the wild hills to the west of it.

Rome in occupation of the Vale Royal and of the magnificent corn lands of Cheshire could not neglect the Lancashire lowlands immediately before her, and the occupation of these would further contain the Pennine moors and shut up the raiders within their unfertile territory.

But Rome in occupation of the arable lands from the Mersey to Lancaster and the Lake mountains upon the west, and in occupation of the great plain of York to the east, was in occupation of the two great natural ways to the north, and the north offered not only the Valley of the Eden and all the good land of which Carlisle is the natural capital, but also, beyond the Scotch hills, that belt of lowland between Clyde and Forth which Rome perpetually coveted and yet seems never to have been able to hold in a really permanent fashion.

The two efforts went on together—the effort to reduce the Brigantes in their Pennine fastnesses, and the effort to colonise the far north. The first attempt, though very lengthy, was at last successful, and the particular mark of its success was the building of that great wall from the Tyne to the Solway which cut off the Pennine hill-men from the

---

* It was the type of battle of which Malplaquet is the modern instance, so far as position is concerned.

barbarians of the north. Four generations of men saw the continuation of the struggle, but it was at last successful. The last revolt of the Brigantes was made under Julius Verus in the middle of the second century, and from that moment one may regard the whole of Britain south of the great wall as definitely subjected to Rome.

The proposal to extend the Roman area by yet another district and to push the frontiers to the Clyde and the Forth, as it was begun long before the final subjection of the Pennines, so continued long after that date, and occupies with varying fortunes the whole of the remaining story of Rome in this island.

It was as early as the year 80 that the same attempt was made, and Agricola made it. He not only attempted to bring civilisation in a permanent fashion to the lowlands of Scotland as far as the line of the Forth and Clyde, he pushed northward, fought a battle against the islanders at some unknown place not far from the estuary of the Tay, caused the country to be circumnavigated, and even had thoughts of an expedition against Ireland. But immediately succeeding upon this first attempt a renewed rising of the Brigantes and the necessity of concentrating in the north of England seems to have wiped out all that Agricola had done. It is not well to be too certain. Agricola had established a line of forts between the Clyde and the Forth "where Britain is narrowest." We have no proof that these were abandoned, but, on the other hand, so far as inscriptions and coins are concerned, we have no proof that the north was then held. What argues most strongly against the holding of the north so early is the building and garrisoning of the great wall, which was made first of turf and, many years later, rebuilt of stone. It would seem certain that the expense of men and material in the establishment of such a line would not have been undertaken had a contemporary effort been in progress to hold the much easier and shorter line between the Forth and the Clyde. And the reason it was difficult or impossible to hold the Scotch lowlands was of course the intervention between them and the last British plains of all that great mass of hill and moorland which vied with the Pennines themselves as a reserve for rebellion.

Less than twenty years after Hadrian's visit, however, the government of Britain in the reign of Antoninus Pius made the second attempt to hold the lowlands. Agricola's whole line was greatly strengthened. A turf wall with its great ditch ran from Carriden to Old Kilpatrick, from tide to tide, and in those forty Roman miles no less than ten forts were established, while we must believe from the evidence that at the same time the great road from the south reached its final extension.

There were two avenues to the north as we have seen: one through the Plain of York, the other through the Plain of Lancashire. That through the Plain of York afforded the easiest and the most obvious communication for troops. Upon it was established the great military capital of Britain, York itself, the seat of the Ninth Legion. Throughout its length, until within two marches of the wall, it passed through a land of ample provision. It was concerned with no considerable obstacles, crossing the rivers of the Humber system by a series of bridges at Doncaster, at Castleford, at Aldborough, which required no great effort in construction. Beyond the wall it passed through Risingham, High Rochester, Eilden upon the Tweed, and so across the hills to the Forth. One great engineering work, the crossing of the Tyne in tidal water at Newcastle, did not lie directly upon this line and, as I have said, there was no principal obstacle in the whole of its trajectory.

It was otherwise with the western line of advance. There, between the Pennines and the Irish Sea, was present one of the most formidable strategical obstacles in Britain—the Marshes of the Mersey—and it is of the utmost interest to note the way in which the work of the Roman engineers at this point determined point after point in the future strategical history of Britain. Between the hill country and the mouth of the Mersey the line as the crow flies is just over forty miles, and over the whole of that forty miles, with the exception of a hard gap two, or at the most three miles wide at Stockport right up against the hills, runs that barrier of marsh which was spoken of in the last chapter as the barrier of Lancashire. It was this barrier which the Roman engineers bridged after a fashion which, from their time onwards for over a thousand years, and right on to the Civil Wars, determined the marching of armies up the western side of the Pennines. For the first sixteen miles as the crow flies, or somewhat over twenty by the channel of the river, the broad and tidal estuary of the Mersey formed a complete barrier. But at the point of Warrington that estuary is already no more than a river, though the marshes on either side are formidable to a marching force. At that point, Warrington, the Romans threw across a great causeway whose line is still marked by the place name *Stretton*, characteristic of such made ways. But though this was the most direct route up to the north from Chester it was necessary to have a communication also with the Stockport Gap which had been the immemorial marching road of the tribes.

Immediately next to that gap and holding it was the fortifiable and perhaps already fortified position of Manchester, in a triangle between two rivers and, if it were properly garrisoned, closing all attempt of an enemy to pass through the Stockport Gap between the marshes and the hills; or, again, if the Warrington Causeway were in the hands of an enemy, permitting an outflanking march to proceed by the Stockport Gap.

It was essential, then, to connect with that road which should lead northward from Chester, not only the passage of the Mersey marshes at Warrington, but some direct line to Manchester. This line was driven from the junction at Northwich. The road north from Chester first crosses the Weaver at Northwich (a salt depot, by the way) and then splits into two; one branch goes over the causeway I have mentioned to Warrington, the other passes by yet another causeway higher up, over yet the same marshes, direct to Manchester. It has left in a place name the record of its passage, for, just as Stretton marks the crossing of the Mersey marshes by the Warrington Causeway, so does *Stretford* mark the crossing of the same marshes by the causeway leading to Manchester. To complete the strategical triangle there must have been a third road from Warrington to Manchester. It has disappeared, and perhaps Chatmoss has swallowed it up.

From Warrington to Lancaster, and so to Overbarrow, ran a road which, north of Wigan, has mainly disappeared. From Manchester by way of Ribchester to Overbarrow also ran a road which we can still trace. From this point, Overbarrow near Kirkby Lonsdale, a single road led northward. It followed first the valley of the Lune precisely as does the modern railway, and using the same pass as does that railway. It had a station at Lowbarrow Bridge, whence it descended upon the Valley of the Eden, crossing Revensworth Fell, and striking for Kirby Thore across that river. Thence, down the valley to Carlisle, it can be clearly followed so far as Birrens, across the Scotch border. Thence afterward it totally disappears. It does not follow, as antiquarians too often presume,* that the line was not continued to the Clyde. The disappearance of Roman roads in a puzzling and incalculable fashion over hundreds of miles is a matter I have had to deal with

---

* Birrens is the last station marked in the Antonine Itinerary, but as the Antonine Itinerary is no pretence to a complete road map of England, and as we do not know its date, that evidence is of very little value.

often elsewhere, and without confusing so short an essay as this with numerous instances, it is enough to say that no negative evidence will ever convince a close observer of the Roman road system that a route which cries out for military communication had none such;—though all evidence has disappeared. But, at any rate, we have no proof of direct communication with the Clyde by a regularly engineered Roman military way over the great moors which separate the Scotch lowlands from the Solway. Having thus grasped the nature of the approach to the north and the great part it played in the road system of Roman Britain, we may end with a brief view of what happened to that attempt to hold the Scotch lowlands in a regular fashion. We have followed that attempt as far as the building of the forts and of the wall from Forth to Clyde, just after the year 140. How long this second attempt to hold the Scotch lowlands continued we cannot tell. Inscriptions give us at least forty years, but do not carry us beyond the reign of Marcus Aurelius. The vague presumptions of antiquarians would lead us to believe that the northern extension was abandoned by regular troops (save in the close neighbourhood of the Tyne and Solway line) at some time in the last twenty years of the second century. In the first years of the third there was another expedition into Scotland, and from a phrase used by one historian we must believe that, at that moment, the line from Forth to Clyde was still regarded as the boundary of the Empire.

The truth is, of course, that the general civilisation of Rome had already overflowed her military boundaries. Wild barbarians might raid a frontier district, but the mere fact that there was something to raid proved that the culture of that district was Roman. Further strategical knowledge of Roman Britain we have none. The north was, in the fourth century, continually raided, and as continually the raids were repelled. It is possible that the reconstructed Valentian Province was a military recovery of the Scotch lowlands, but we have no proof of it.

The new factor coming at the close of the period which determines the strategical topography of all the Dark Ages is the approach of enemies by sea, and not of civilised enemies coming by sea across the Straits of Dover or the Channel, but of barbarian enemies coming by sea from the west and from the east.

Unfortunately, precise documents and all remains and relics from which inference could be drawn illuminate us so little upon this new phase of British strategical topography that we cannot pretend to deal with it as we have dealt with the civilisation of Britain by Rome.

Indeed, the whole story of the 600 years and more which follow the breakdown of Roman central government in Britain is, upon the military side, a story so barbaric and so ill attested that we can only mark its largest lines. Still, those largest lines are clear enough and are determined by three points.

First—the rivers are still obstacles to inland marching, but have become, in a predominant fashion, *avenues of invasion into the country*.

Secondly—communications other than the rivers penetrating the country (and that mainly from the east) are, in the main, the surviving Roman roads, to which we must add a certain revival of the old British trackways.

Thirdly—the points which are the objectives of a barbarian march, both on account of their wealth for loot and of their defensive capacity, are the points established by the long period of Roman civilisation.

With the great discussion upon the political extent and nature of the early pirate or "Saxon" raids into the Roman province of Britain we have here nothing to do. It is enough to know that, from about the end of the third century (more than a hundred years before the central authority of the Empire abandoned this island), those auxiliary troops which everywhere tended to coarsen or break up the old scheme of civilisation, were being brought into Britain from the inland Rhine and from the marshes at the mouth of that great river. Meanwhile, at the same time or a little later, pirate raids were falling with increasing frequency upon the eastern seaboard, and these, generically known as "Saxon," started naturally from the shores just outside Roman influence upon the Continent: districts which would be acquainted with the wealth and opportunities for loot afforded by a Roman province, which had profited by some tincture of Mediterranean commerce and invention, but not sufficiently civilised to effect of themselves a direct incorporation with the Roman system.

Two other continual attacks were being made upon our Roman province, one from the west by the Irish over the sea, one from the north across the wall. But neither of these two others are of lasting effect or carry with them any lesson in strategical topography unless it be that the Caledonian or Pictish raids came to nothing because they had mainly to deal with the barren lands of the north; the Irish raids came to little because they had to deal with rivers that did not carry them far inland, and often with a mountainous and sterile coast. The advance of the eastern invaders, on the other hand, whether in the form of Frankish or Frisian auxiliaries and mercenaries, or of pirates from the North Sea, bore fruit because they dealt with all that segment of the island of Britain already well settled and developed by the Romans, from hills bounding the Yorkshire Plain on the north-east to Dartmoor and Exmoor on the south-west, with a projecting tongue of good soil running into Cheshire and Lancashire, which is one continuous habitable land full of harvest.

Of the lengthy but unrecorded struggle connected with the first pirate raids, the two principal effects were the degradation of civilised life and the slow transformation of the language; and in their welter two main chapters succeed each other. In the first, which must have been very brief, the pirates approach in successive bands from the sea and fight up *inland*, following the rivers. In the second you have a sort of promiscuous fighting between the numerous kinglets who divide the land—some certainly native; some as certainly pirate; more of whom we cannot say what origin they had—and all contending one against the other without pause, and with no apparent result.

This chaos, which necessarily followed upon the disintegration of society, lasted for at least one hundred and fifty years—till the end of the sixth century. We have no record of it and no better material than late and distorted legends whereby to judge it.

The re-admission of Britain to some sort of civilised life after the first pirate raids comes with the arrival of the Christian missionaries from Europe. Written record reappears, and the origin of our new history is roughly coincident with the year 600. For two centuries more the disorderly welter of fighting within the island can at least be followed though hardly explained. There are at least records, though few and unarranged, and we have a few main dates and places of which we can be sure. We have, moreover, an historian—Bede. There are no fresh pirate raids—until the second period of these disasters opens with the ninth century. The first appearance of these "Danish" raiders is, roughly speaking, 800.*

---

* The first Viking Fleet touches England in 787—at the earliest, or by another version, at the latest 793. The first one to touch Ireland is recorded in 795, and though England proper enjoys an immunity of over thirty years after the first raid, 800 is a convenient date to take as a turning point.

The "Danish" raids can no more be reduced to a series of strategical plans than the "Saxon" ones of two centuries before. But at least we have some record of them, and we particularly note how the great Roman roads remained the chief communications of the island. Thus, in the first great battle between the pirates and the Christians, the Battle of Ockley, you have the pirates coming up the Thames and sacking London and Canterbury (though what the "sacking" of London may have meant is doubtful), and then marching from London Bridge down the Roman Stane Street to Ockley* in Surrey. That was in 851.

Twenty-seven years later, after the Danes had overrun the mass of the Midlands, their decisive defeat at Eddington in 878, at the hands of Alfred, was again received within a few miles of the great Roman road running westward from Salisbury to the Bristol Channel; indeed, it was upon that road, just where it leaves the great Ridge wood, that Alfred camped on the night before the battle.

The second division of the Danish Wars, in which they were dynastic and had a direct political object—the placing upon the English throne of Scandinavian princes—opens in the year 982. It proceeds again from the coasts and the rivers sporadically enough. You have—at the very beginning—the ports made objects of attack; Chester, London, and Southampton. Again no united strategical plan of any kind appears, unless it be found in the instance of Swegen's invasion of 1013, when, from the Humber and York he marched with deliberate intention against the south, raiding the whole centre of England. But even here the thing is little more than ravaging a belt of country with the hope of striking terror into those who govern it.

Even the great struggle of Edmund Ironside against the invaders is strategically meaningless; a succession of battles, fought with no enduring effect by such forces as he could bring to action, now with success, now with ill-success—never with a result or a political decision. But even in this random business the fighting and the marching proceed by the Roman roads or the older tracks, save where the Danish fleet compels an issue near the coast and far from such ways—as at Ashindon in Essex. Thus the battle of Sherston is just off the Fosse

---

* The site of this battle has been disputed—as most things have been—by the scepticism of our time. For the argument in favour of Church Oakley in Hampshire, see the Proceedings of the Hampshire Field Club for 1904, and Professor Oman's England before the Norman Conquest, page 425.

Way, that of Otford on the old road from Winchester to Canterbury, that of Brentford on the great Roman way from London to the south-west.

Throughout the establishment of a Danish dynasty, the later expulsion and the return of the House of Wessex with Edward the Confessor, there is no regular campaign to record.

It is not until the Norman Conquest, more than six centuries after the ruin of Roman Britain, that a regular order returns to warfare in this island, and that its plan is susceptible once more of description and analysis.

CHAPTER III
THE NORMAN CONQUEST

As a piece of mere strategical history the Norman Conquest merits but a short study in the military history of England; for though as a political event it ranks second only to the great turning points in the story of Europe—the Roman occupation of Gaul, the conversion of these islands to the Faith, the expulsion of the Moors from Spain—as a *military* study it is too simple and too brief to merit on its own account any lengthy description. It contained but one general action, Hastings, the strategy leading up to which was of the most obvious kind, and the strategy succeeding which, though masterly, was elementary in character. In the years that followed the hardest fighting was concerned with nothing more scientific than the suppression of isolated rebels, its great marches were devastating raids. It gave rise to no conspicuous siege-work, nor to any interplay of opposing forces long drawn out.

Nevertheless we must make of the Conquest a fundamental study if we are to understand English military topography, because it illustrates at once those three main points in the military topography of England upon which I have insisted on a previous page, and also is the origin of that feature in our military history which marks the whole of its domestic fighting down to the seventeenth century:—those three main points are the obstacles of the Thames, of the Pennines, and of London, while the feature which the Conquest originates is the establishment at a great number of scattered points throughout the realm of separate strongholds—*castles*—round which, as checks to an enemy's advance, depots of supply, bases for excursion, and refuges for forces in the field, all the subsequent history of warfare in Britain turns for four hundred years.

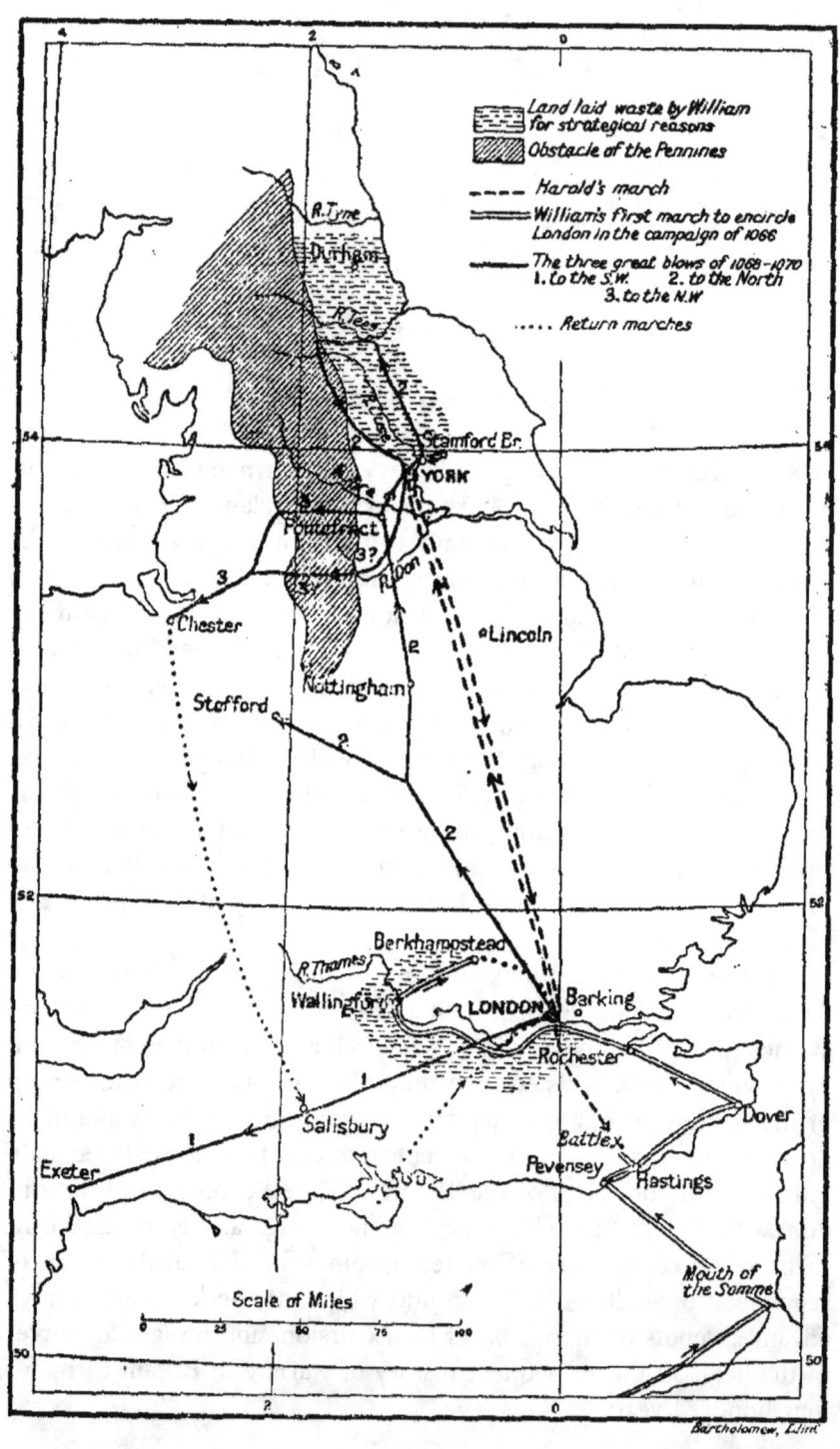

Some description of the type of society which William was attacking would be useful to a comprehension of the Conquest. In so short a space as I have at my disposal it must be enough to say that it was identical in all its main features with that same Feudal society of the Continent whence the Conqueror had drawn his forces and upon which he modelled all the exact legislation of his reign; it was identical with the rest of Western Christendom in religion, morals and social concepts. All Europe was then of the same stuff; a vague, hardly conscious instinct of unity survived in Britain as it survived in Gaul. But the social fact on which men were most clear and to which their affections, their fears and their daily habits were attached was the dependence of a number of free men each upon his lord, and the whole host formed by the gathering of such lords, supported by the agricultural labour of the great mass of the people who never entered the field and who were not yet in law technically free, though centuries of Christian influence had long ago destroyed the servile basis of that old Roman civilisation whence the eleventh century society of England and of France had both proceeded.

On this account we must never look at the struggle between William the Invader and the opponents whom he met upon English soil as a national struggle. In the first shock William at the head of a feudal host met Harold, the accredited and crowned King of an English feudal system. The two men were fighting for what each claimed as a personal right. When, after the first decisive action the personal claims of Harold were overthrown and he himself killed, William had to meet no national resistance, but only occasional and sporadic rebellion, provoked in one place by the personal ambition of a powerful feudatory, in another by the irritation following upon administration in a foreign speech and the disturbance of an old settled order; in a third by the mere opportunities for brigandage which the confusion of the Invasion caused. To this it must further be added that the society of England in the eleventh century, though framed upon the same model and, as I have said, of the same stuff as that of Gaul or of the Rhine Valley or of Northern Spain, was less closely knit and somewhat less regular in structure: a feature which added to the lack of consecutiveness and plan in such chance resistance as the Conqueror had to meet after the Battle of Hastings.

These political points have no concern with such a study as this save in so far as they affect the strategy of the campaign.

That strategy, directed against no cohesive opposition (after the first great battle had been decided), had none of the simplicity of plan which we have seen to mark the Roman advances from the south to the north of the island, for it was not designed to break down in a methodical manner a united resistance.

The Campaign of the Conquest resolves itself into two clearly marked portions. The first occupies the autumn of 1066. In it is finally decided William's claim to the throne; its effect is his formal crowning at Westminster. This was the political object of the invasion. Once it was successful the ultimate success of all subsidiary action was assured.

The second portion of the Conquest consists in his march towards the extreme and somewhat isolated south-west, with the reduction of a rebellion in Exeter: it was not called for until two years after the first decisive movement had been made. It was followed by a march along the great road to the north involving very little fighting and doing little more than show the King's presence in Yorkshire and along the line of the great Roman way between that district and London. Next year, 1069, a rising in the very places where the Conqueror had shown himself (a rising aided by the Danes) was followed by a renewed approach of the Conqueror, his complete subjugation of the northern strategical centre of which York was the stronghold, and a wholesale wasting of the land standing again to the north of this between Humber and Tees.

The third of the great fighting marches in this second stage of the Conquest consisted in a stroke to the west across the Pennines and the capture of Chester. With these three blows, entirely successful, the one to the extreme south-west, the second to the north along the great strategical line east of the Pennines, the third west across the Pennines, to Chester and the gates of the country on the north-west, the Conquest was completed, and no military episode follows save the envelopment and destruction of an isolated valley in the Fens.

I

The first and decisive phase of the Conquest in the south-east was as follows:—

Harold was crowned and enthroned at Westminster upon Twelfth Day, January 6, 1066, in the morning of that day at High Mass. William gathered a great host of his own feudatories, a lengthy business involving negotiation and persuasion. Attracted by promises of gain many of the Gaulish feudal chiefs who were independent of his overlordship (including chance comers from beyond the Alps and the Pyrenees), built a great fleet, which after a first assembly on the central coast of the Norman duchy proceeded eastward and lay weatherbound in the estuary of the Somme, and against the threat of it Harold gathered his forces in the south of England.

It is possible that if the shock had come during these preliminary manœuvres, and if William had crossed in summer, the first decisive action might have favoured Harold. But the invasion halted, and the same wind which kept it bound upon the French coast, brought to the north of England, Hardrada, with a fleet of 300 galleys. He came to aid (and it is typical of feudal society) Harold's own exiled brother Tostig. The local force awaiting this northern invasion under the two northern earls, brothers, Edwin and Morkere, covered York upon the south two miles from the walls of the city.* Upon the 20th of September they were utterly defeated and the Scandinavians were in the northern capital. But meanwhile Harold was marching north at top speed to meet this new danger. He left the south unguarded; he made the Isle of Wight his station of observation, but his fleet, which had also watched the southern shore, was exhausted, and it had had to go round into London river a fortnight before to refit, losing many ships upon the way, for it was beating up against north-easterly gales.

At this point the reader should note a rapidity of movement which proves the existence and maintenance of made ways and the continuity of the great Roman roads in this island.

On Sunday the 24th of September, Harold was at Tadcaster with his forces. The advance had not, indeed, proceeded all the way from the south coast, for before it began Harold had retired upon London, but even so the distance from Tadcaster to London was a matter of close on 200 miles by the great road to the north, and Harold covered that in nine days. He entered York on the morrow, Monday the 25th, and at Stamford Bridge upon the same day, where the main eastern road crosses the Derwent, seven miles from the city, he completely broke the northern invasion.

---

* The fight was at Fulford over the river opposite where the race-course stands to-day.

But that march and that victory decided history in a very different fashion from the mere repulse of the Scandinavians. In that same week the wind veered south, favoured the fleet of those other invaders which was waiting in the mouth of the Somme, blew it across the channel, and three days after this fight at Stamford Bridge, on Thursday, September the 28th, William landed at Pevensey.

Two points must now be seized by the reader. The first is a repetition of that rapidity of travel which I have already insisted upon. The second the clear plan which William had evidently made for the decisive fighting in the south-east. The first may be briefly told. Harold could hardly have heard of the landing until Monday. He managed to be in London (not, of course, with his whole host, but in person) upon the Friday, or at the latest upon the Saturday. That was good riding. Allow the longest limit and it means four full days and part of two others in which to cover 200 miles. But excellent as the feat was, what follows is perhaps more remarkable. The mass of the army (which was of course on foot), after that fine march north of 200 miles in nine days, covered the same distance in the same time southward again, with that great fight of Stamford Bridge in between. The host was actually marching *out* of London upon Tuesday, October 11.

It is worthy of remark that no army in this island has covered such a distance in such a time since that date. By the evening of the second day he was in position before the Norman host and standing upon the defensive, his forces drawn up upon the crest of the round hill called ever since that time "Battle Hill";* and this last feat had been the greatest of all, for the army had covered nearer sixty than fifty miles in those forty-eight hours, and that over worse country by far than the great northern road which had permitted their rapid dash to the south. This splendid achievement was, however, yet another cause for defeat. The levies of the northern shires could not follow so rapid a march, nor had those of the west come up when the issue was decided.

The second point, the clear plan which William must have laid, is evidenced by the site for which Harold had to make before he could come in touch with the invader.

---

* I forbear to trouble the reader with the word "Senlac." The place is so called in Odericus Vitalis. It is no more a Saxon name than Bergerac, but is probably the misrendering by a Gascon scribe of a local Sussex name. According to some authorities this name might be that of "Sautlache," a place within the limits of battle and one whose title may mean "the sandy stream."

Why do we find Harold on the evening of that Friday, October the 13th, thus stationed at two hours' march from the south coast? It was because William had deliberately refused to leave the immediate neighbourhood of the sea. He had brought his fleet on to Hastings from Pevensey and beached it. He had occupied Hastings, throwing up earthworks both at Pevensey and at Hastings to protect his supplies; nothing moved him from his determination to hold fast by the sea—neither the comparatively near neighbourhood of London nor the cruising in the offing of Harold's fleet, which had been ordered to cut off a retreat by sea. For more than a fortnight he stood his ground, and his reason for doing so was his determination to fight a decisive battle within immediate touch of his supplies, as far as possible from the bases of reinforcement which Harold could command, and so situated that if he won it he could immediately subdue the entries into the island from his own dominions, and if he lost it he should yet have an opportunity for retreat to his ships.

The decisive action was immediately joined; upon the morrow, Saturday, October the 14th, Harold's host was destroyed. What followed was the prosecution of that clear plan which, as I have said, William certainly had framed from the beginning of his expedition. Though there was now nothing in front of him he marched not upon London but upon Dover, took the town and castle and thus now held the main communications between his ultimate base upon the Continent and the land he had invaded. This done, he follows up by the Roman road to Southwark, appreciates far too well the nature of the obstacle of London to attempt a capture of so great a town with his forces (it was far larger than anything which his soldiers would have had to deal with upon the Continent, its walls defended an area quadruple that of contemporary Paris or Rouen). He contented himself with burning the southern suburb and then marched right up the south bank of the Thames, making no attempt to cross at the numerous crossings from Brentford onward, whether by ford or by bridge, but deliberately harrying the country to the *west* of his way, far into Surrey and Berkshire. His motive was gradually to encircle and cut off that great strategical obstacle and political centre, London. When he should have reduced it by such a strategy it would give him not only kingship but supplies, the chief group of population in the kingdom and the great passage over the Thames, with its control of the nexus of communications between the north and south of the island.

Not until he had got abreast and more than abreast of London upon the west, right up to Wallingford, did he cross the river. Having crossed it he made straight for Berkhampstead, and when he reached that place he had thrown round London a ring of wasted land only unenclosed towards the east. At Wallingford came his first political success. He there received the submission of Stigand, the archbishop of Canterbury.

He continued that strategical ring of devastation throughout north-east Oxfordshire, proceeding apparently along the Icknield Way throughout central Bucks until he turned through the gap that now serves both the railway and the Grand Junction Canal, and came upon the authorities of the kingdom at the fortified point of Berkhamstead. He had not yet cut off London from the great northern road or from the east, but he was easily in striking distance of the great northern road—a day's march off and not two hours' march from the Watling Street. Within two days London would have been isolated had he continued. At Berkhampstead then, the great earls, the clergy, and, most significant, a deputation of the citizens of London gave hostages, swore allegiance and offered the crown.

It will be seen from what has been said how clear, simple, and successful was the strategy which decided the campaign of Hastings. One might add that after his crowning upon the Christmas Day of that year, William was not without military design when he withdrew to Barking to hold his winter court. He stood there in command of the eastern road, and it is not fantastic to suggest that this last residence of his before crossing to Normandy, was a completion of the circle he had thrown right round the great military obstacle, communication and base of supply which London had been for so many centuries and was to be for so many centuries more.

II

The strategics of the three great blows, south-west, north, and north-west by which William destroyed the few sporadic rebellions against his now admitted claim to the feudal kingship of the island can be briefly told. Indeed the term "strategic" is too dignified for so exceedingly simple a matter. No true armies marched or manœuvred against him, no true siege of any fortified place was necessary, and wherever the Conqueror went (accompanied, be it remembered, now by great masses of native troops as well as by the remains of his continental levies) he was immediately and absolutely successful.

During an absence in Normandy which ended with the midwinter of '67 there had been sporadic outbreaks of men outlawed or disappointed. And in the attempted anarchy foreign aid had been asked for and in part obtained. The feudal chief of Boulogne had helped an assault upon Dover, which had it succeeded would have been really serious, but it was easily beaten off. Exeter in the extreme south-west was the first point to which the Conqueror on his return was called to march. The reason of its discontent was a peculiar one characteristic of the loose feudalism of England before the Conquest.

Merchants had no objection at all to paying William's taxes or owning allegiance to him as King, but they seem to have desired the constitution of a free city with autonomous jurisdiction within its walls. The novelty they would not admit was a garrison. William marched against them, aided now by great bodies of native troops, took it within three weeks, and with that chance and not considerable encounter the whole of the south and south-west is quiet.

The next stroke was to the north. (It will be noticed how all these uncertain attempts were at a distance from the seat of government.) Edgar, the heir of the House of Wessex, but recently reconciled with William and given a high place at his Court, had fled. A storm drove him to Scotland. The Scottish King offered his aid to place him upon the throne. The Bishop of Durham joined the conspiracy, the Norman garrison of the town was massacred. Upon the news York also massacred its garrison. William marched northward at once, re-occupied York and quelled the movement. But this was not the "blow towards the north" to which I alluded. That came the next year. Durham and Northumberland William had not visited. They were held to him by an oath on the part of their chief men and by nothing more. A second insurrection followed upon William's departure. Edgar, the heir to the old throne, once more appeared from Scotland. William came back for the second time. For the second time re-established his authority, but for the second time neglected to march beyond Tees. For the second time he left the north to attend to piratical attacks upon the south-east coast in support of the sons of Harold, but they were defeated without the necessity of his presence, and those heirs of the dead King fled to Ireland in the summer to be heard of no more.

Then came the third outbreak in the north aided by the Danish fleet. For the third time the Norman garrison fell with its castles. The real danger to William in this third and most serious insurrection was not the isolated and doubtful bands following native feudal chiefs, but the Danes. Their ships lay in the Humber, their armed men occupied the north of Lincolnshire.

It was William's third march north against them and the insurrection which they supported, which I call his second blow, for it was much more in the nature of a campaign than either of the two first. He proceeded leisurely enough, garrisoned Stafford and Nottingham, waited for three weeks at Pontefract before crossing the Aire, by one account because the river was swollen, but much more probably because he was negotiating with the Danes. He took York easily enough by assault. Garrisons were reinforced, and once again he held his Christmas Court in that northern capital which was of its nature the strategic centre of the north. What followed was a military execution of a terrible sort, but informed by a very distinct military purpose. William determined to put a buffer between the plain of York, which was now his northernmost limit, and that border country with Scotland beyond it from which he must expect, if he did not take due precaution, ceaseless and embarrassing raids: for that border country was now and remained for centuries a disputed land, the lords of which, under the conditions of the day, could hardly be held in hand from the southern centres of government. William determined not only to establish his defence by the method of devastation, but to establish it at once, winter though it was, and systematically all the arable land between the Yorkshire Wolds and the Pennines, from the left bank of the Ouse up to the Tees, from the Tees up to the Tyne, he utterly wasted.

The whole population of Durham fled to the islands off the coast, save such as were cut down in their flight, and they were thousands. He burnt every steading and destroyed every implement his hand could reach. The chiefs submitted, the greatest of them was permitted a marriage into the Conqueror's family, and while his men raided Northumberland the King himself returned from the Tees, not following the road of the plains by which he had come, but showing himself and his power, in spite of the desperate weather, up in the Yorkshire dales, which are the foothills of the Peninnes. This last was a desperate venture in which the army was almost destroyed by the climate, and William himself once lost. It might have wiped out, had it finally gone ill, the effects of the last three years, but the Norman determination conquered. He came back to York with a loss of nearly all his horses but with an armed force still surrounding him.

There was a third thing to be done. He had not shown himself in the western plain which lay beyond the Pennines. There on the Welsh marches was a perpetual danger from the alliance of the insurgents with the mountaineers, and from the proximity of the sea, with its opportunities for Irish and for Scandinavian fleets.

It is remarkable that in spite of the late and terribly severe season he marched not round the hills but across them. His blow was the more sudden and the more effective. He started in the beginning of March and, though we do not know his route, we must presume that it lay along the old Roman road that uses the Skipton Gap, unless he went to the south by that other Roman crossing which connected Glossop with the plain of the Don. At any rate, the forcing of the high hills in such weather was more than the foreign contingents could bear, though to the native troops it was more endurable. His continental soldiers grumbled and attempted mutiny. His personal example of sacrifice and endurance quelled this outbreak, as did that of Napoleon in the Guadarrama centuries later in weather much the same. He took Chester, fortified it, receiving the submission of Eadric, who had led a whole series of local raids; marched down to Salisbury and there disbanded the army. The Conquest was complete.

III

The third strategical feature of the Conquest is one of permanent moment to the future history of England. Wherever William established a garrison and occupied a town of any size or a strategic position of any value, he built a castle.

What permanent fortifications had existed previous to the Conquest, save in the shape of town walls, it is not easy to determine, but certainly they were at once ruder and far less numerous than those which the Conquest and the generation following it deliberately established.

It would be impossible within the compass of this to make even an incomplete list of the great works of this sort which marked the period, but it is of the first importance, if we are to understand the military history of the succeeding five centuries in the island, to grasp the nature of this revolution.

We have seen what the character in strategics of a stronghold is. It is a refuge, a base, a depot, and an obstacle all at once. When a country is covered with such points the great lines of strategy tend to disappear and warfare must be largely composed of the attempted reduction by one body to the struggle of such strongholds as may be held by the other. An army cannot pass in safety between neighbouring fortified castles if they are upon a scale sufficient to maintain a considerable force. Even, therefore, if the history of the succeeding centuries had contained examples of regular invasions, the planting all up and down the island of these great works would have profoundly modified the story of those invasions and we should never have had the simple lines of action which mark the Roman and the Norman subjugation of the land. Supposing, for instance, that William, after his reduction of Dover immediately following upon the Battle of Hastings, had found upon his line of march garrisoned points at Rochester and at Windsor, to the south of him at Reigate and at Guildford, to the west of him at Oxford, and in front of him at Towcester and at St. Albans (as a later invader would have found them), and supposing these garrisoned points had had their garrisons well munitioned with supplies within their defences, that sweeping circular march of his which isolated London would never have been possible.

I say that even regular invasions would have been disturbed and modified by so great a system of internal fortification.

But, as a fact, the military history of England in the next four or five hundred years is not one of invasion, but of civil war, and in conflicts of this sort it is obvious that the existence of a vast number of defended and garrisoned points scattered all over the territory of conflict must determine the nature of that conflict entirely.

A vague and general strategy is to be extracted from each phase of all history, as we shall see. There was something of it even in the Barons' Wars, and something of it in the Wars of the Roses, but the main feature of all the fighting from the Conquest onwards is the determination of its lines and results by the system of castles which the Conqueror and his immediate successors established.

The work was gigantic. Many of these fortresses were upon such a scale that they could maintain a considerable garrison for months and defy all operations save that of a regular siege. Even the lesser works could check the advance of an enemy for many days, and there was hardly a market town with its supplies of provision and missiles, hardly an important river crossing or pass over difficult hills that was not guarded with permanent works of stone, duly surrounded by one, two, or even three walls, and ditches, carefully supplied at any expense with water, and provided with such curtains of resistance as rendered it possible to compare that vast undertaking with the system of defended towns which cover the frontiers of the seventeenth century, or even the system of entrenched camps which are the mark of European defence to-day.

I have said above (and illustrated my remark with a footnote) that it would be impossible within my limits here to make even an incomplete list of the known works of the period, but a few examples will illustrate what I mean. Consider the whole of the south coast. There was not a gap through which a landing force could proceed unless the castles were friendly, unoccupied, or reduced. From Dover to Rye and Winchelsea, from Rye and Winchelsea to Hastings, thence to Pevensey, to Lewes, to Bramber, to Arundel, to Chichester, to Porchester, to Southampton run a continual string, no two of which are more than a day's march one from the other. They are backed with subsidiary works at Winchester, at Salisbury, at Farnham, at Guildford, at Reigate, at Rochester, while immediately behind their line you have the later works of Petworth, Amberley, Knepp, Hurstmonceaux, Bodiam, Canterbury.

We are accustomed to think of these places now as ruins or as the seats of chance wealthy men, and to think of them in the past as the private refuge of individual commanders who held them with a sort of possession. But in their original intention they were within the domain of government, they formed the military scheme upon which government depended, they were garrisoned for the King under leaders of his own appointment, revocable, and mere offices of state.

I wish that my limits would allow me to insist upon this capital matter in the military story of England. To show the line of the Thames held by the Tower, by Windsor, by Reading, by Wallingford, by Oxford; the Welsh marches contained by Newport, by Monmouth, by Hereford, by Ludlow, by Shrewsbury and by Chester; the gap into the Vale Royal by Beeston; the Midlands by the complex of Northampton, Bedford, Towcester, Huntingdon, Warwick, Nottingham, Leicester and twenty others. The great road to the north was blocked successively from Hertford march after march at Stanford, at Grantham, at Newark, at Lincoln, at Gainsborough, at Doncaster, at Pontefract and at York. Every port was defended, every obstacle of water held at its passage. My limits do not permit me this, but I have said enough to emphasise what this enormous business of castle building did, and how it formed a framework for five centuries of warfare.

CHAPTER IV
MEDIEVAL WARFARE—I
THE CAMPAIGN OF MAGNA CHARTA

All the fighting in England between the Conquest and the Civil Wars of the Commonwealth was of a domestic character with the exception of the expeditions against Scotland and Wales, to which I shall refer briefly at the end of this book.

While one might distinguish at least half a hundred chapters in the course of these six centuries (1066–1651), five separate and clearly defined campaigns, or series of campaigns, especially mark the period. These are the civil war under Stephen in the middle of the twelfth century; the insurrection of the Barons against John at the beginning of the thirteenth, which may be called the Campaign of Magna Charta; the insurrection of the Barons against Henry III in the middle of the same century; the Wars of the Roses; and, lastly, the Civil Wars themselves in the seventeenth century.

Of these five salient episodes in the domestic warfare of England the first four fell in the Middle Ages. I propose to deal, therefore, with everything before the struggle of Charles I against Cromwell under the title of Medieval Warfare.

As all that warfare was between parties both present in the island, and not between natives and foreign invaders, it suffers from the confusion necessary to all civil struggles, but particularly accentuated in the case of our history by that factor of the numerous *castles* upon which I insisted in the last chapter.

All four medieval episodes—that of Stephen, of John, of Henry III and of the Roses are, nevertheless, susceptible of a certain arrangement, betray a certain strategical plan, and are capable of logical discussion in a survey of military history, with the exception of the *first*.

The first episode, I say, the struggle between Stephen and Matilda,

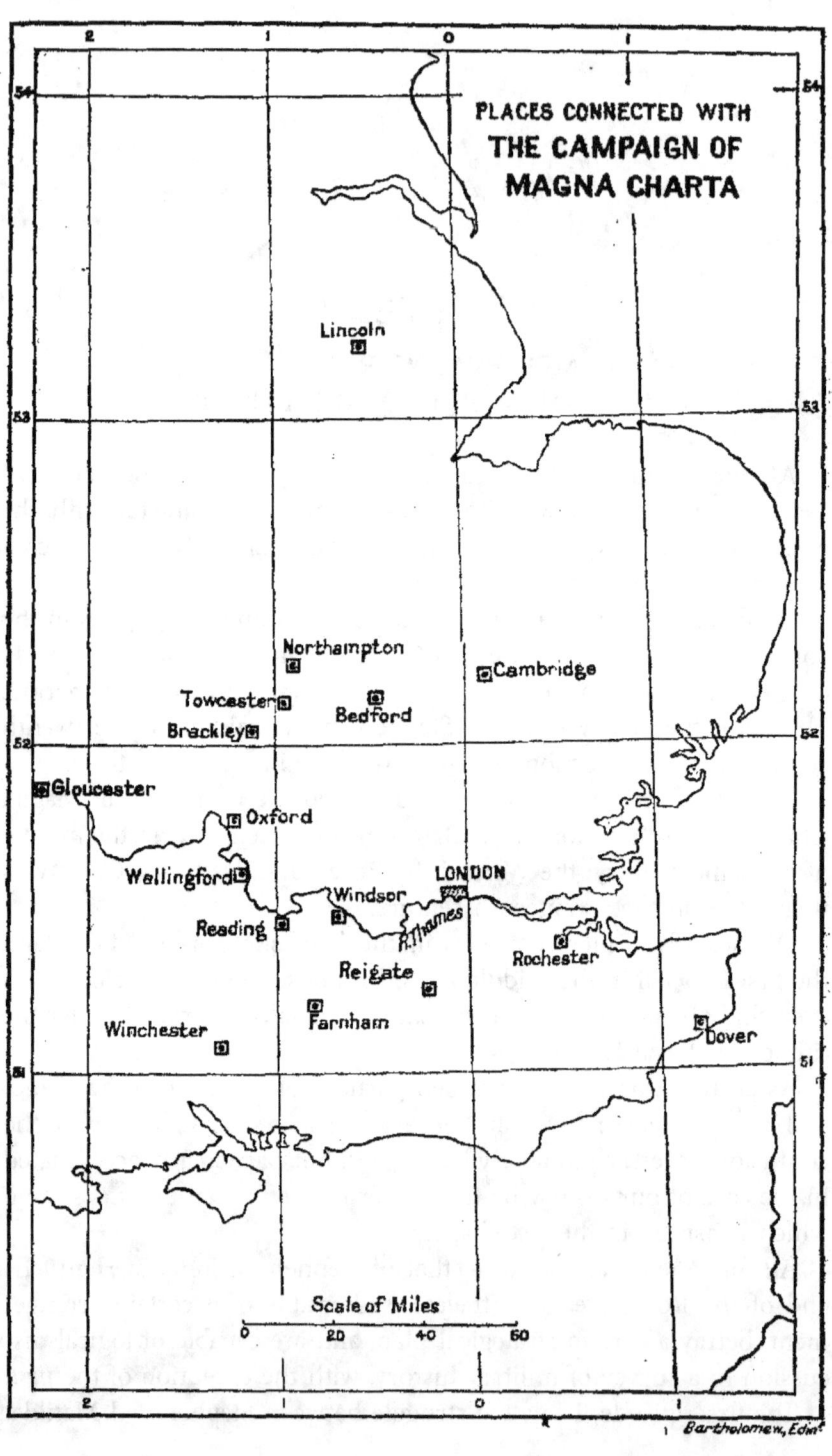

it is impossible to submit to any arrangement. It was a mere anarchy of powerful feudal chiefs, each in actual (though not legal) ownership of certain strongholds and in legal as well as actual ownership of vast military resources, each warring against his neighbour in pairs, or in small groups, and all changing and re-changing sides with bewildering lack of consecution. One can no more establish a logical sequence in such scrimmage than one could establish it in a hand-to-hand fight at a public meeting. It is best, therefore, for our purpose, to omit any attempt to analyse the confusion of Stephen's reign, and to proceed at once to the more regular and far more interesting conflict between John and his Barons which I have called the Campaign of Magna Charta. Here a great soldier was pitted against good metal, and his plans were recognisable and clear.

The pivot of the Campaign of Magna Charta is the great castle of Windsor: and the castle of Windsor as (*a*) the terminal of the Thames line of works, (*b*) the chief royal garrison within striking distance of London.

The hill of Windsor had suffered Roman occupation, whether fortified or not we cannot tell. During the whole of the Dark Ages, with their absence of central government and their looseness of organisation, its admirable opportunities had been neglected. It was left for the Conqueror to seize those opportunities, to effect a purchase (or rather an exchange) of the site with the monks of Westminster, its former owners, and to establish a great fortified position upon the hill.

Let us see what those advantages were. The great road from London to Winchester passed over the Thames at *Staines*. The Thames was itself throughout the Middle Ages not only an obstacle but a highway. Staines was, therefore, a nodal point of capital strategic importance. But Staines had not in its immediate neighbourhood a position defensible after the necessities of medieval defence.* The nearest such position was the hill of Windsor, and the garrison of Windsor was little more than an hour's march from the passage of the river at Staines. It therefore cut that passage.

---

* By which I mean this: an abrupt acclivity, or patch isolated by marsh, yet with an approach. In the Roman days, with a disciplined infantry, one could defend a mere ridge upon the flat. To-day, with long-range weapons, the immediate approaches to a defence count less. In the Middle Ages the type of assault demanded for defence the obstacles of acclivity, of marsh, or of water, and the presence of one narrow approach, natural or artificial.

The road direct to the west crossed the Thames opposite Maidenhead and ran through Reading. The garrison at Windsor were within two hours' march of that crossing, within half an hour's of the nearest point on the western road.

For defence upon the north and east the position had a precipitous bank. The approach from the south was through a district devoid for nearly a whole day's march of supplies. Again, any attempt to approach London from the west, south of the Chilterns, was blocked by Windsor. Finally, Windsor was one long but quite possible day's march from London, and it was the end of the line that held the lower river. It formed with a second day's march to *Reading*, a third day's march to *Wallingford*, a fourth's from Wallingford to *Oxford*, the terminal of a chain of castles which between them blocked the whole line of the Thames between London and its upper branches. The Campaign of Magna Charta divides itself into two phases.

In the first the Barons, manœuvring against their king, turn the scale against him by receiving in aid that great strategical factor of *London*, which we have seen by its size, wealth and position so largely to determine the course of English warfare. They obtain John's consent to the Charter.

In the second—after an interval of some months—foreign aid is called in by the Barons, but John, by his superior military capacity, is already victorious when his chance of complete success is lost in death.

As to the first, what we have need to note most carefully is the all-importance of the four Thames castles for the king and the all-importance of London for the Barons.

It was in the summer of 1214 that John's last attempt to retrieve his continental disasters which, more than any oppression of his at home, had given the great nobles their cause of offence, was crushed at the battle of Bouvines.

In the following January, a conspiracy having already been formed against his rule and an oath against him taken in particular by the nobles of the north, John came to a truce with the conspirators and fixed Low Sunday, the 26th of April, as the date upon which the truce should end.

On the Saturday before Palm Sunday, that is, on the 11th of April, 1215, the nobles gathered a force numbering anything from 2000 to 3000 men-at-arms—which would mean from 10,000 to 12,000 all told in their command. Their object was to win the independence of the great feudatories from the central government, and to decide for the moment in their favour the perpetual medieval struggle between oligarchy and a popular monarchy. Though that success might mean the calling in of foreign aid and even a submission to a new dynasty, they would pay the price.

When they had mobilised this force they began to converge it upon *Brackley*; their motive for choosing this point I will set out in a moment.

With what total forces John could meet this menace we cannot tell. But they were excellently trained and well-paid professional soldiers, largely of continental origin, and distributed as garrisons in the great

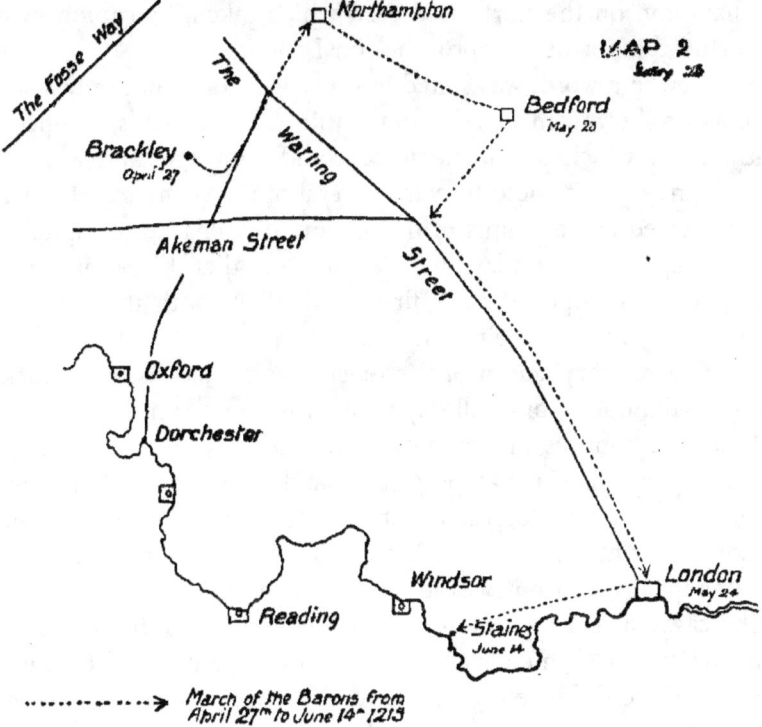

castles upon which he depended during the coming struggle. Particularly did the King amply furnish with provisions and men the four great castles which held the line of the Thames, though many other garrisons, as we shall see, held other isolated points, and in particular must be noticed Northampton and Bedford. Of those castles upon the line of the Thames the King himself held Oxford.

Let us begin by contrasting the two opposing strategical positions at the beginning of the struggle.

What was the importance of Brackley?

Its importance lay in its command of a whole group of roads and in the power of a force situated there to strike at any one of a number of fortified sites still in the hands of the Crown. Brackley was within an hour's march of the Portway, another hour's of the great Roman road from Dorchester to the Watling Street, not a day's march from the Akeman Street, and within striking distance, though a full day's march away, of the Fosse Way; and marching down from it one could intercept any attack on London from the west. It was but a day's march from Oxford itself on the south, from the royal stronghold of Northampton on the north and east: which taken, its captors would command the northern approaches on London.

Brackley, in a word, was suited in every way to be, not only a shield for London, but, from its situation within a net of roads, at once the centre upon which a suitable force could converge, and a starting point from which it could threaten several of the enemy's castles while it still covered any attempts of that enemy to menace the capital.

It was upon the Monday, the 27th of April, that the Barons assembled at Brackley opened their first negotiations with the King who, from Oxford, refused their demands.

The first military action of the rebels was to march from Brackley upon Northampton, one full day's march to the north and east.

Their object in this sudden movement was to begin with the capture of the garrison of Northampton, the paralysing of one after another of the King's isolated forces, and in particular to hold the approaches on London from the north. As for the line of the Thames, they would not attempt it because it was too strong for them.

The castle of Northampton resisted for two weeks. Its resistance is characteristic of all medieval warfare in this country and of the way in which these defensible posts decided the main issues of combat.

Despairing of reducing it the Barons, still keeping in mind the necessity of covering London, which was their principal political support and would prove an invaluable basis of recruitment and supply, marched on Bedford. That post was yielded to them by treason.

Hardly were they within its walls when, upon Saturday the 23rd of May, they received an urgent summons from the leading citizens of London, who may have feared, from the distance at which the Barons' army now found itself, an advance upon London by the King from the west.

That advance had not as a fact taken place. The characteristic position of London throughout the whole of this struggle should be noted as much as that of the castles. It was too hard a nut for any medieval soldier to crack—even a Plantagenet—and none ever cracked it.

Upon receiving this summons the feudal cavalry of the Barons made a single astonishing march. They struck east for the Ermine Street on the Saturday morning, marched down it all that Saturday and all the following night, and entered the city upon the Sunday morning, May 24th, having covered in one ride well over fifty miles. What that must have cost in the exhaustion of the horses, how their footmen straggled and tailed in, we can guess, though we have no record; but London could re-supply and re-mount a very much larger force, and though the Tower was still held by a garrison of John's, it is again characteristic of the military position of London in the Middle Ages that the garrison was shut up behind its defences and would attempt nothing against the town which had now definitely joined the rebels.

It was the active defection of London (the sympathy of whose great merchants was already known to be strongly against the Crown) that put John at this early stage in the campaign in a position so inferior to his enemies as to make it necessary for him to treat.

Of the garrisons along the Thames he left *Oxford* for *Windsor*, and thence upon the 8th of June sent a dispatch to the Barons in London asking for a parley. They marched out, fully armed, along the Roman road to Staines; and in a field immediately beyond the crossing of the river (according to the best judgment, for the site is not certainly fixed), Magna Charta was presented and assented to—but what followed was a recovery of his military position by John and a piece of fighting upon his part so well planned and so successful, that nothing but the accident of his death prevented its final triumph.

In the first place the king appealed to Rome against the promise he had given to those wealthy rebels, and he appealed upon the plea that it was no true contract because it had been gained by force, and meanwhile he temporised with the aristocracy and the great London merchants who had risen against him, pretending that he would soon execute his side of the treaty and ever postponing that duty.

In such a deadlock passed the summer of 1215. He set to work methodically to recover the whole of his military position. He sent to the Continent for well-trained mercenaries and received them. He recaptured Rochester Castle which he had given over to the aristocracy as a hostage. He garrisoned castle after castle all up and down England with the hired men who kept coming to him through the ports which he controlled—and especially Dover with its castle—and, had he been left to struggle against his Barons, each without allies, he would, by this policy of garrisoning point after point all over the country, have at last contained the rebellion in a sort of net in which it would have been enveloped and destroyed piecemeal.

In their desperation the rebels were willing to alienate the northern counties of England to the Scotch Crown. John met that threat with all the energy of the Plantagenets. He ravaged the north as his grandmother's grandfather had ravaged it. He set fire with his own hands, in the morning, to whatever steading he had billeted himself upon the night before, and he pushed up into the border with a thoroughness that even William the Conqueror had not shown. His advanced bodies almost reached the gates of Edinburgh. They burnt Berwick, they burnt Haddington, and they burnt Dunbar. In all the north two castles alone remained in the hands of the rebellion when this cruel and terrible, but militarily most effective, task was accomplished. But John's immediate success had been met by a counterweight: his adversaries had called in Louis, the heir apparent to the French throne, and the father of him that was afterwards the Saint, and had offered him the crown of England. Louis had accepted it. The French invaders began to pour in with the end of the year 1215 and in the January and February of the next year. Louis himself landed upon the 21st of May, 1216.

It is from this point and during the five months following that you may seize the capacity of John as a general. How much he depended upon the national irritation against the proposal of the Barons to place a new dynasty upon the throne, and against the much more lively hatred of foreign nobles following that invasion, it will be difficult for a modern critic to determine. The whole of that society was, in its government, French-speaking and of a French culture.

But undoubtedly the mass of men that were born within the island of England, whether of the French-speaking nobility or of the now English-speaking peasants (for you may almost call their language

English), had begun, by this summer of the year 1216, to rally round the traditional throne of the nation and the Plantagenet claim which that nation admitted. At any rate, whatever we think of the popular position, the campaign was masterly well fought by John. The reader must concentrate his attention upon two points: Windsor, commanding all the western approach to London, and the terminal, as we have

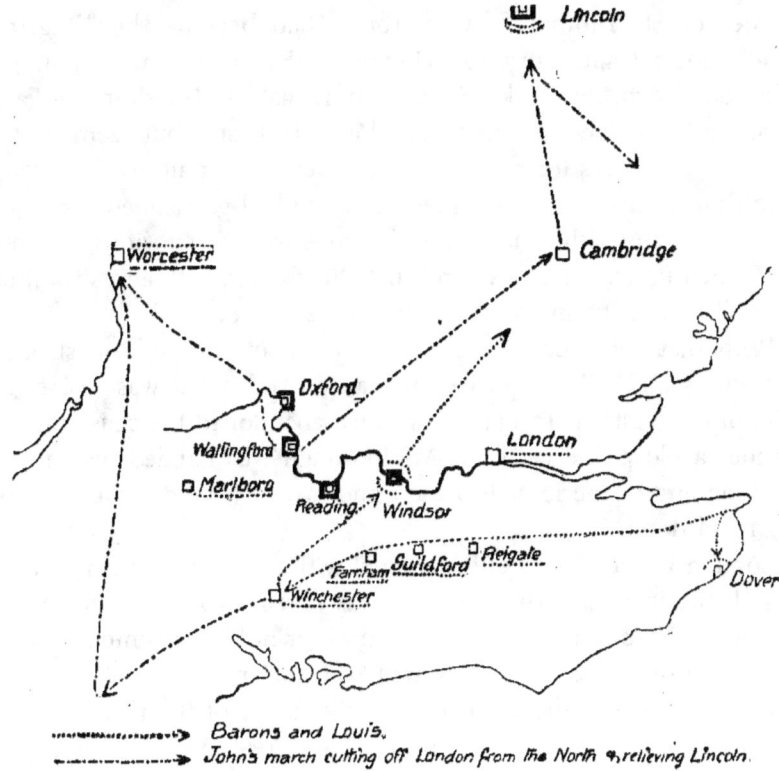

··············▶ Barons and Louis.
── ── ──▶ John's march cutting off London from the North & relieving Lincoln.

seen, of the Thames line of strongholds; and Dover, whose castle held the immediate line of supply from the Continent, whether from friend or foe. It was John's garrisoning of these which permitted him to come so near to a final success, to provide by his efforts for the continued rule of the Plantagenets in England, and, though that was not consciously his purpose, for the separation in history of the French and English crowns: a matter of vast import to Europe. He was a great soldier.

At the beginning of the business one might have thought John's position hopeless, considering that the Barons had now the reinforcement of an unlimited supply from France, and behind that reinforcement the powers of the strongest government in western Europe. And, as a fact, John was compelled to retire and to retire precipitately before the advance of Prince Louis, the ardent support which the merchants of London gave to the foreign invader, and the fierce determination of the rebels.

Prince Louis marched right down the old road (which, since the murder of St. Thomas of Canterbury, had become the "Pilgrims' Road") from Canterbury to Winchester. He landed at Stonar, just below Sandwich.* He took the castles of Reigate, of Guildford, of Farnham. John may have meant to stand at Winchester, but seems not to have had the forces for resistance there, seeing that all his best troops were shut up in the many castles which he had garrisoned.

It was on the 14th of June that the three weeks' victorious march of the French Pretender ended, and that Winchester, with all its tradition of English sanctity and government, surrendered.

With that surrender came the defection of such of the stronger nobility as had still supported his cause. And, what was worse, the chief of the western strongholds in turn abandoned the cause of John without a blow. The castle of Marlborough was handed over to the rebellion and to the French prince, and Worcester did what Marlborough had done.

London was against the Plantagenet with nearly all the chief nobles and all the invaders. The situation was saved, as I have said, by the line of the Thames and by Dover, and never did the all-importance of the system of castles in English medieval warfare appear more clearly.

Philip Augustus, the French King, the father of the man who was now attempting the English throne, had a great eye for country and for the main elements of a strategic problem. He was, perhaps, the chief soldier of his time. He had urged upon his son the necessity of seizing *Dover*, with its castle, before anything else was done, and it would have been well for Prince Louis had he followed his father's advice. Now that the whole of the south and west seemed to have fallen into the hands of Louis's party, that prince turned somewhat too late to the reduction of the Dover castle, the defence of which denied him a monopoly in the communications with the Continent.

---

* Dr. Stubbs calls it Ston*or*, a small error but very irritating when it comes to indexing, particularly as nearly every other authority calls it Sandwich.

As so often happens in the strategical history of a failure, the brilliance of previous successes concealed from the party of the French invader and the Barons the fact that they had lost their opportunity. When John had retired from Winchester it was to the south that he retired, into Dorset. The King of Scotland had not only reappeared in the north but had been able to march right down to the south of England unimpeded, renewing that claim which John, a few months before, had so fiercely destroyed, and, indeed, no contemporary observer could have imagined anything but the approaching destruction of the House of Plantagenet.

But Dover held out. It held out under the command of that Hubert de Burgh whose great part in the salvation of the dynasty I could wish to linger upon, did this little book concern itself with the political history of England. While Dover held out tenaciously, Windsor held out as well, and between them these two defences determined the issue of the campaign.

For one thing, time was gained by these prolonged defences—and, indeed, to gain time is the chief object of fortification. Among other effects of that delay was the formation of associations within the counties, farming men who began to resist the foreigners.

Again, the resistance of Dover and of Windsor permitted the recovery of Worcester, which the King's forces reobtained in the course of July.

In the month of August, while the army of the Rebellion and the Invader was sitting down hopelessly before Dover, and while Windsor with magnificent tenacity had destroyed all hope of assault against it and had turned the efforts of the besiegers into a mere blockade, John moved. He went right up from Dorset through the Valley of the Severn, and down again to make certain of a western line, limiting and framing the efforts of his opponents. Next he did what convinces us of his grasp. He got right across eastward so as to draw a northern limit also against the power of his enemies.

London, remember, he could not touch. London was, throughout the Middle Ages, as I have said so often, the inviolable point. But when he had constituted a western limit against the foe, and then a northern limit beyond which London and those whom London supported could not strike, he would have confined the enemy to the south and to the east of England, and from the bases of the north and of the west he could recover his realm.

It was with the end of August that he marched right for the line of the Thames. It was no chance blow. He knew what the effect would be. By the time he had reached Wallingford, the third of the line of fortresses commanding the river, and was evidently heading eastward, the besiegers of Windsor grew alarmed.

It was the Count of Nevers, the French commander, who seized the nature of John's move. He appreciated what the raid across the north of England to the east would mean: the cutting off of London from the north, the isolation of the successful invasion and of the successful rebels from the whole of England save the south and east and, if Dover still held out, a grave peril in the matter of supplies.

There was a sort of race as to which should get control of the northern roads and, as always happens in converging movements of the sort, the better trained army won. Both were making for Cambridge. John got there first, although from Wallingford to Cambridge is at least one long day's march farther than from Windsor to the same point. There have been many such movements in the long story of arms, movements in which two opposing forces are marching not one against the other, but both for one point of convergence, seeing which can reach it first. Who wins in such a race is master, and John had won. By that fine stroke eastward, he had come to control all the northern roads giving access to London, leaving, as we must presume, a garrison upon each. The Barons had lost the move. They went back to help the force before Dover, and in that strategical defeat of their enemy the family of Plantagenet had secured a continued inheritance.

For what followed was no longer of great consequence. A force of the Rebels and of the French prince's was besieging Lincoln, the fortress and depot flanking the road between north and south. Now that John had cut off London from the north, that siege was easily raised. His march down south again, through Lincolnshire to the Wash, might have led to a thorough reconquest of the south had he survived, but immediately after effecting it he died (whether by poison or how will never be known) at Newark, upon the 19th of October, 1216.

As has so continually happened in the history of strategics and of warfare, the foundations of success had been so securely laid by one good move that subsequent disasters, even the death of the general himself, could not undo their effect. Within the week of John's death, Dover surrendered.

The coronation of his nine-year-old boy not a fortnight later at

Gloucester, without a crown, with a mere band of gold, hardly with ceremony and, as it were, a Pretender, was, nevertheless, the coronation of a man destined to reign over England for a lifetime. I say again, the House of Plantagenet was saved, and it had been saved by the great eastern march of the King just dead.

For now it was no longer morally possible that the Invader, or that the Rebels, or the Scotch King, should between them dismember England. John was in his grave, but he had won. And he had won as a strategist.

Louis garrisoned, after his enemy's death, Norwich and Colchester and Orford (then a great port—its traditions are still amazing), but he was doomed. In the May of the following year a last attempt of the Invaders upon Lincoln was broken. A national fleet held the Channel in the same August, cutting off Louis from France; in September, less than eleven months after John's great march and death, Louis, by the Treaty of Lambeth, abandoned his claims and, in a phrase which ought not to be forgotten, though its appearance at so early a date is a trifle rhetorical, "England was England."

CHAPTER V
MEDIEVAL WARFARE—II
THE BARONS' WARS

The next clear episode in the story of medieval warfare in England takes place nearly fifty years after the campaign of Magna Charta, and is the rising of the aristocracy, or at least a principal part of it, against Henry III. Of that rising *Simon de Montfort* was the leader, and it is intimately connected with the development of the English Parliament upon the model of the earlier Continental Assemblies.

With the politics of the period this study can have nothing to do save in so far as they afford an explanation of its military side: and in this aspect they are exceedingly simple. The political object on the one side as on the other was to obtain control of the executive machinery of the country, of the power of issuing writs and garrisoning fortresses. To effect this the victor in a decisive action in particular desired to obtain custody of the person of the King: and it may almost be said that the varying fortunes of the campaign turned upon the capture and recapture of Henry III's body. Of such moment still was the executive power of the hereditary monarch.

The period of operations is a short one. After a very long preliminary stage of political discussion covering several years, Simon de Montfort committed the first acts of hostility in the second week of June 1263. He fell in battle, and the effort of his party terminated, upon the 4th of August, 1265.

These twenty-six months are divided, as to their military aspect, into three quite distinct phases.

(1) There is a preliminary phase of no military importance save that it brings Simon's army into the field and inaugurates a state of war. This phase covered the last six months of 1263. It was succeeded by a truce and by a consent of both parties to arbitration.

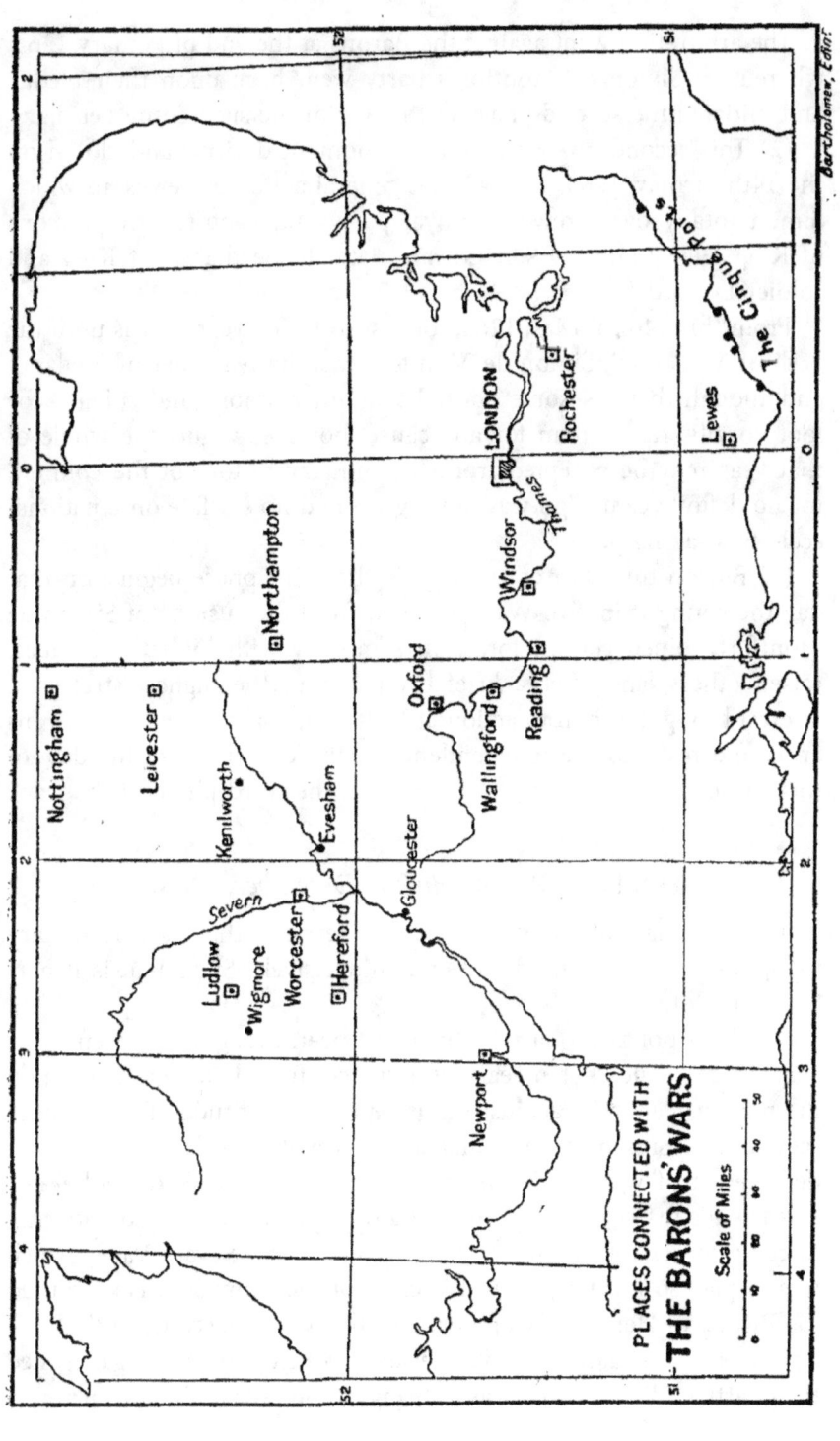

The arbitration went against the Barons at the end of January 1264, whereupon Simon de Montfort's party went back upon their pledge and initiated the second phase of the war in the succeeding February.

(2) This second phase was for the moment decisive and closed on the 14th of May, 1264, with a great general action at Lewes, in which Simon totally overthrew the Royal party and captured the persons of King Henry and his son Edward, later to be that great King and soldier Edward I.

From this 14th of May, 1264, for just over one year, that is until the 28th of May, 1265, Simon de Montfort was the real ruler of England, and though-there is some sporadic fighting among individuals, for loot, locally, rather than for any cause, however vague, the whole of that year may be excepted from the military history of the country, for no definite campaign was in progress and no warfare on a national scale was taking place.

(3) But on this 28th of May, 1265, the third phase begins: on that day the young Prince of Wales escaped from the custody of Simon de Montfort, joined certain forces in sympathy with his father's cause, raised others, and after a brief campaign of the highest strategical interest brought Simon to action at Evesham, completely destroyed his army and restored the independence of the Crown. With the date of this battle, the 4th of August, 1265, ends the third phase of the war.

The First Phase (*June to December*, 1263).

The first phase of the war is of little interest in the study of military topography. It is confused and ends indecisively. Such as it is it may be briefly told.

The long political quarrel which had been dragging on even in its acute stage for nearly ten years, culminated in so definite a stand upon the part of Henry III against the independent attitude of the aristocracy and of Simon in particular as to provoke the latter to the first definite act of war. De Montfort raised an army of feudal adherents and friends (as yet unsupported by any popular levies), and with that force he successfully struck at the west and at that Severn Valley which was to play so great a part in the close of the campaign. He captured the Bishop of Hereford, a supporter of the King's party, upon the 11th of June; he took Gloucester, Worcester, and Bridgnorth and garrisoned their castles. His next step was to bring in the factor which recurrently determines the issue of military operations in this country during the Middle Ages: the obstacle, the base of supply, and the nodal point of communication which are all summed up in the word *London*. He marched straight from the west upon the capital.

The attitude of London is not so easy to determine from contemporary witnesses as it would be were those witnesses less partisan. But it may be laid down with fair certitude that if certain of the very greatest merchants desired, probably for the sake of peace, the maintenance of the King against the rebellion, the mass of the commercial interests in the town, certainly the mayor, and to a very large extent the populace (which, in the thirteenth century, were, it must always be remembered, a powerful economic body of small owners, strongly organised in co-operative associations), were actively in favour of De Montfort.

The effect of this attitude upon the part of London was immediate. Royal troops held the Tower, but the possession of the castle had no such effect in the case of London as it had in the smaller towns; it carried with it no control over the immensely larger population of the capital, nor any power of commanding its supplies and wealth. The Prince of Wales did manage to raise a sum of money—not, indeed, from citizens as a whole but from the Temple only—and having done that his first care was to march out of a hostile centre far too large for his forces or those of his father to subdue. Once again, therefore, as we have to note perpetually in the story of English warfare, London acts as a virtually autonomous military element, and the scale into which it throws its weight preponderates. Edward withdrew his forces to Windsor, and the value of the opinion of London was further proved by a skirmish to the south of the river in which Simon, though at the head of a very small force of armed men, was saved by the opening of the gates of the town to him, and his retirement within its defences.

With Edward garrisoning Windsor and a large Royal army in the field, with the Barons' party reposing upon London as a base, all the strategical elements with which we are already familiar were present for a great struggle upon the lines which had been followed in what I have called the campaign of Magna Charta fifty years before: the holding of the line of the Thames: the struggle for the key to continental communications, which was the castle of Dover: individual sieges of the other strongholds, and particularly of the castles that commanded the great northern roads leading into the capital.

But no such struggle, as a fact, took place at that moment. On the contrary, a truce was arranged, as I have said, and both parties consented to submit the quarrel to arbitration. The arbitrator chosen was St. Louis, the King of France, the son of that man who had attempted to obtain the English throne in the campaign which I described in my last section, and who but for the military energy of John would undoubtedly have attained his object.

No man in Europe commanded, or perhaps has since commanded, the universal respect which St. Louis enjoyed in this middle of the thirteenth century. No man was more permeated with that conception of government which satisfied the happy and stable society of the Middle Ages, nor could the decision of any other man be compared to his for the integrity upon which it would be founded. When, therefore, it was decided to submit the question to St. Louis, general opinion foresaw a certain cessation of the struggle, a cessation that would be the more certain when St. Louis' sentence should have been confirmed at Rome.

With this arrangement, to which both sides were pledged, ends the first and somewhat confused phase of the struggle.

The Second Phase (*January* 1264 *to May* 1264).

What St. Louis had to decide was whether certain large concessions which Henry had made to the aristocracy some years before, which he had recently refused to confirm on the plea that they were wrung from him by force, were to stand or no. The French King opened the Arbitration Court at Amiens; its sentence was no compromise between the two parties, but a perfectly clear declaration for the King. It restored to him the plenitude of his power, summoned his vassals to return to their allegiance, and in particular proposed to curb the particularist pretensions of the great feudatories and notably of De Montfort, which were abhorrent to the morals of a time especially jealous of the encroachments of the great against the general control of those new national monarchies which all Europe now regarded as the guarantees of popular liberties. This decision, which is called the Mise of Amiens, was issued upon the 23rd of January, 1264.

For a full comprehension of what followed it would be of advantage (if I had the space) to describe for the reader the character of De Montfort. I must content myself with presenting to the reader the picture of a man made after a model not unfamiliar to those who have studied the various types of the Gallic temperament when it is affected by military ambition.

Brutal in discipline, of an indomitable physical tenacity which could force him to endure more than all he imposed upon his followers, perpetually considering death, and above all persuaded of something sacred in his career and capable of informing with a sense of mission any object of arms he had before him, Simon de Montfort repeats what half a dozen of the northern French leaders in the First Crusade exhibited, and what you may later find in the recovery of France from the Plantagenets, in the Wars of Religion, and conspicuously in the enthusiasms of the Revolution, with its mystical creed and its enormous and permanent achievement.

It was his personality around which the next eighteen months of fighting were to turn: his ceaseless confidence in a divine selection, and his fierce insistence upon religion in his forces, between them determine the character of the struggle: his corresponding lack of equity, which was all merged in fanaticism, drove him and his: his eye for arrangement and for chance made him in particular a leader of cavalry.

Consonant with the character of such a man came, after the Mise of Amiens, an immediate repudiation by him of his own pledges. The Barons again gathered their forces, the Royal party was again compelled to defend the King's claim under arms.

Very few days passed between the receipt in England of the news that St. Louis had decided for Henry, and the first blows struck by the rebels. Already in the early part of February 1264, the perpetual border fighting on the Welsh marches was made a pretext for the seizure by the party of De Montfort of certain Royal castles in the west. Henry came back from France (where he had attended the Court of Arbitration) upon the 15th of February, to find himself face to face with an enemy already in the field.

The strategical elements of this new struggle were as follows: The Cinque Ports with their castles—that is all the southern entries into England by which the approach from the Continent could be made upon London—were with Simon, and London, of course, was still very strong in support of him. Rochester, the great castle breaking the road between Dover and London, was, however, garrisoned by Royal troops; so was the line of strongholds upon the Thames. Henry summoned a conference between himself and his foes in March at

Oxford. Simon came to it but only to announce his determination upon continuing the war.

Upon the 3rd of March the army of the King, true to that strategical conception which required whatever party in a war had London against him to cut London off from the north—the same strategy as

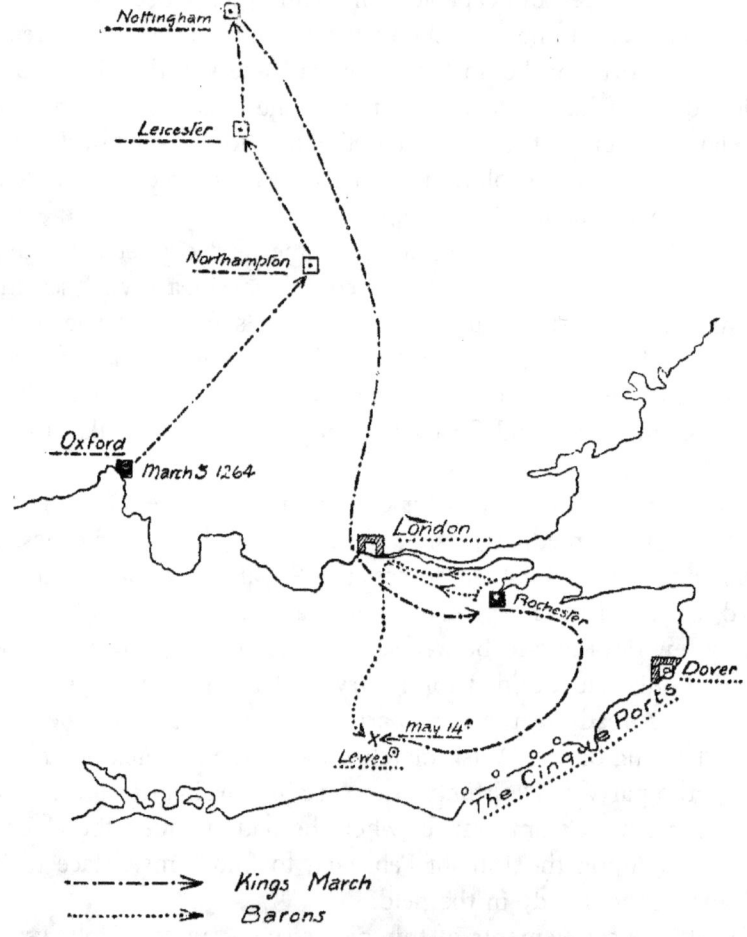

had determined King John to make that great march of his eastward from Wallingford—took Henry's force from Oxford eastward and northward also, so as to cut the approaches to London from the rest of the island. The move was successful. The three strongholds that commanded the approaches from the north, Northampton, Leicester, and Nottingham, were successively taken.

While the King thus secured the line cutting off London from the north (we have seen that he already held the Thames line cutting off London from the west), the Barons, to secure the whole of that south and east wherein they already possessed London and the Channel ports, laid siege to Rochester, the one garrison which blocked the main road between Dover which was theirs and London which was theirs. The Royal army having secured the northern fortresses marched back round London into Kent to relieve Rochester. They succeeded in relieving it.

These movements were over by the beginning of spring, and the Royal army as it left Rochester which it had relieved, found itself marching through that south-east of England which was the enemy's, and necessarily drawing against it from London Simon and his forces.

The King might have attacked any one of the seaport castles and have attempted a gradual reduction of the coast. To have done so would have been to isolate London entirely, and to have made certain his ultimate success. He was prevented from pursuing such a plan, by the immediate necessity of meeting in the field a great force which De Montfort had levied against him. That force was not even for the bulk of it a force of feudal knights. It was swelled by great levies from London and even from certain other towns: it is the presence of these which lends some countenance to the historians who maintain that Simon had a true popular backing.

Against the approach of so large a body it was impossible for King Henry and Edward, Prince of Wales, to attempt the prolonged siege of any one of the coast castles, during which operation they would have certainly been caught by the enemy in force. Observe, therefore, that it was the backing which London gave to the rebellion which determined all the last strategy of this campaign.

King Henry came up the Vale of Glynde to Lewes. From Fletching, close at hand, Simon de Montfort both sent and accepted challenge, having marched down so far from London. This was upon the 12th of May. Upon the 14th the two armies met upon that open slope of chalk turf above Lewes where the racecourse now stands, and between that site and the steep escarpment of the Downs to the north. The result of the encounter was the complete defeat of the Royal army, the capture of the King and the Prince of Wales by the leader of the rebellion, and his consequent mastery of England.

From the evening of Wednesday, the 14th of May, 1264, Simon could and did issue writs in the name of the King, his captive, whom he carried about with him. He garrisoned all the Royal castles and for a year ruled England. So ended the second phase of these hostilities.

The Third Phase (*May* 1265 *to Aug.* 1265).

The political events of the year elapsing between the Battle of Lewes and the resumption of the war (from May 1264 to May 1265), have little concern for us: but two matters personal to the military leaders must be grasped if we are to understand the sequel.

The first of these is that the strongest feudal chief in alliance with Simon de Montfort was the Earl of Gloucester, and in the course of the year that very powerful noble, with a great body of feudal dependants and one might almost say subjects, in the Severn Valley, quarrelled with the head of his party.

The second is that Simon de Montfort held in England the feudal position of Earl of Leicester, and had, not as his private possession (for all fortresses were still regarded as properly the strongholds of the Crown), but none the less as a place of habitation and a family centre, the castle of *Kenilworth*, a few miles north of Warwick. This point, though purely domestic, turns out to be of great importance in the ensuing campaign.

The ceaseless border warfare between local lords, now Welsh against English, now at cross purposes, English and Welsh against English and Welsh, drew Simon as the virtual governor of the country beyond the Severn exactly a year after the Battle of Lewes. He went to impose peace upon the district; he took with him, of course, the captive King and Prince of Wales, with all the power to issue writs and to govern which the presence of the Crown implied. Though, therefore, he had gone so far as Hereford, and was cut off from the rest of England by that Valley of the Severn in which the family of the Earl of Gloucester was supreme, he felt secure.

But on the 28th of May the Prince of Wales escaped from the narrow guardianship which Simon had set over him. Throughout his life this man was particularly remarkable for the promptitude of his military action. He was, in this May of 1265, not quite twenty-six years old, and this soldier who was to be so great in English history after, under the title of the first Edward, inheriting all the rapid decision of the Provençal blood (his mother, from whom his character sprang, was from the south), turned the course of the war.

It was just before sunset of the 28th of May,* that the young man had made his escape. There was a concerted plan arranged for his succour, and that night he slept in the castle of Wigmore among friends, a border castle of the marches garrisoned by the Mortimers.

The next day he met Gloucester at Ludlow, and the armed reaction against Simon had begun.

As for Simon, when, in Hereford and with the King at his side, he heard of the Prince of Wales's escape, he had no clue as to the direction which the fugitive might have taken. He knew that there was some talk of a force coming in the Royalist cause from over sea to the Pembrokeshire coast—they had indeed landed. De Montfort issued writs all over the country, accusing Edward of rebellion and treason, and summoned by the Royal writ feudal levies from all over the kingdom to the Severn Valley. By an accident which has never been explained in so great a commander, but probably because he did not know what forces he had in front of him and wanted to gather all the regular bodies he could before fighting a decisive action, De Montfort remained in that distant western post of Hereford apparently inactive. He secured himself for the coming struggle by a treaty with the Welsh chiefs, which virtually destroyed the claim of the English Crown over them. He even engaged not a small force of Welshmen to join his command, and at last, but very late, after more than a month's delay he moved. Even so he did not dare move towards the Severn. He hoped to turn that line by crossing the Bristol Channel from Newport, and so re-entering South England by the harbour of Bristol, the castle of which was still garrisoned by his men. But while De Montfort had thus lain so strangely inactive, Edward had moved Gloucester to do everything required for success. He had marched all up and down the west recruiting until a very considerable force was raised from lands as distant as Cheshire and the Irish Sea on the one hand, Somerset and the Bristol Channel on the other. They took Worcester without fighting, Gloucester by storm, and after two weeks' siege the castle of Gloucester as well, and they proceeded for the first and last time in English history to make of the Severn itself a true line of defence.

---

* And here, again, I wish I had the space to illuminate this story by a picture: it was on that high ridge of Tillington which overlooks Hereford from the north and west that young Edward saw the single figure issuing from the wood, recognised the signal, and galloped to meet his friends.

My readers will remember on a former page the reasons why alone of our chief rivers the Severn has not played a great part in the military topography of England. It is too shallow and too easily passable for that role, nor does it form beyond a short distance above its mouth a workable means of communication, transport, and supply. But difficult as was the task Edward and Gloucester determined to accomplish it, and, indeed, De Montfort's lingering upon the wrong side of the river could suggest no other course to capable leaders than the attempt

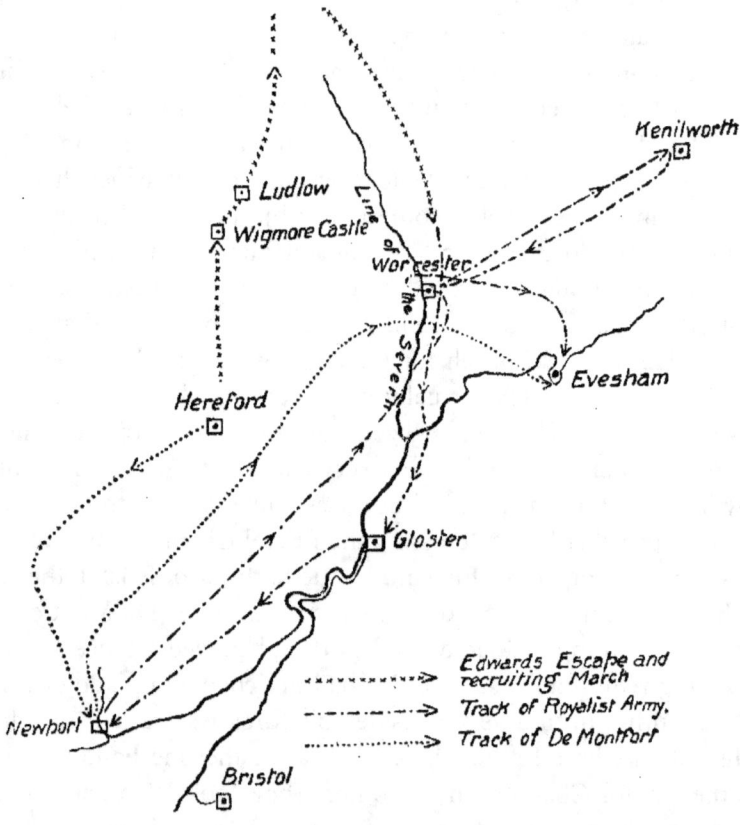

to contain him by holding the stream. The fords were deepened and every one of them guarded, the bridges broken down and, as we have seen, when Simon did move he could hardly move with any hope of success against the obstacle into which the Severn had been made by his enemies. Therefore it was that he struck southward for Newport, expecting transport across the Bristol Channel.

He was disappointed. Edward attacked him at once. Montfort broke the bridge over the Usk, and that obstacle alone saved his army. But he could not cross over to the Somerset shore; Gloucester blocked it and the mouth of the Avon with a fleet, and the man who two months earlier had been the master of England, turned back again into the Welsh hills, still carrying with him the King, and thinking, perhaps, that he would be condemned to a decisive action with his small forces somewhere upon the line of the Severn which his enemies held.

Had he been forced to such an action in such a situation he could hardly have avoided defeat, but, as it happened, fate gave him one more chance.

Among those summoned to Simon's aid by the King's writ was Simon's own son. The writ found him engaged in attempting to reduce the only castle on the south coast which still maintained the Royalist cause. He abandoned the siege and came westward to his father's aid, but made first, whether for recruitment or whatever other cause, for the family stronghold at Kenilworth. He lay there upon the 1st of August. His force was small and was but one of many which Simon had hoped would slowly converge to his aid upon the Severn Valley.

The news that Simon's son thus lay at Kenilworth tempted Edward to one of the few strategic blunders of which he was guilty in the course of a long life of arms. He could not resist the temptation of capturing such a prisoner. He must have known that Simon was hovering round the line of the Severn in front of his own position at Worcester, but he hoped by sufficiently rapid marching to reach Kenilworth, take his man, and be back at Worcester before Simon could take advantage of his absence. As an isolated feat what Edward did was, as a matter of fact, very fine. He covered the more than thirty miles between Worcester and Kenilworth in one night march, captured many of the small force in houses outside the fortress, but missed his chief object; for De Montfort's son, though he also had slept outside, just got behind the walls in time. Edward swept back to Worcester with the same speed as he had shown in his dash to Kenilworth from it; but the interval of absence, brief as it was, had ruined all the careful arrangement whereby the Severn had been made an impassable barrier containing Simon. That soldier took immediate advantage of Edward's short but ill-judged absence to the east; he marched at once for the ford of Kempsey, crossed it in safety, and found himself at last on the left bank of the river. He had evaded a decisive action fought against him under conditions most adverse to his chances, he had now all England before him in which to seek friends and allies, he still controlled the person of the King, he was still the governor. He at once made for the east, intending as an initial step to make for his own castle of Kenilworth, and thither to concentrate or thence to issue orders for a very considerable recruitment; for his army was still small and would be no match for his enemies until he had joined to it those adherents between whom and himself, now that the Severn was crossed, there was no obstacle.

He must, upon that Sunday, the 3rd of August, as his command proceeded in a long file along the first day's march of twelve miles to Evesham, have felt the future fairly secure. A quite unexpected piece of good fortune had allowed him to turn his enemy's line, and he was marching straight and rapidly for those garrisons and centres of government which, through his possession of the King, he still controlled.

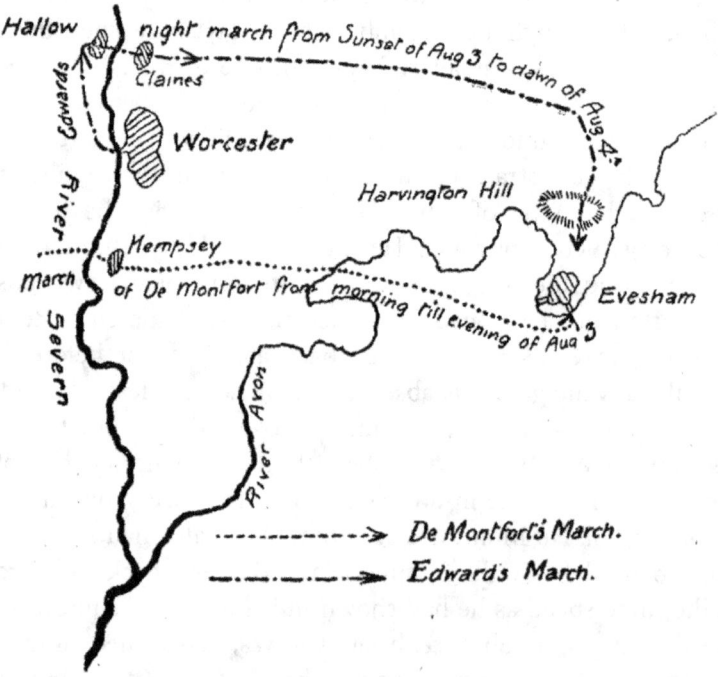

Edward came back to Worcester on that same day. He appreciated how disastrous had been that raid of his on Kenilworth, but he discovered the promptitude to repair it, and what he did is worthy of a close attention, for it is one of the best pieces of military movement in the whole of medieval history.

As the reader will see from the neighbouring map Edward, upon that Sunday afternoon at Worcester, was a day's march behind his enemy. His enemy had got clean away, and the line of the Severn was now useless. How he got it out of his horses and his men we do not know, but he ordered yet another night march, gave it out in the town that he was making for Bridgnorth so that news should not reach Simon of his real intention and, indeed, began his march up the Bridgnorth road upon the western bank of the stream, as though he were looking for Simon's army, believing it still to be there, and ignorant of the crossing which his enemy had effected a few hours before. When the people of Worcester had seen the last of his force disappearing to the north beyond the river, and when whatever of the population which had sympathised with Simon must have imagined that Edward was completely deceived as to his enemy's position, Edward waited for the darkness, and recrossed the Severn under the cover of it by that ford which you may still find, I think, close to the inn that stands upon the bank half-way between Hallow Heath and Claines. He marched right round Worcester through the night, and before the rising of the sun upon Monday, the 4th of August, 1265, he had his men stretched out over Harvington Hill and blocking the road which ran northward from Evesham to Kenilworth.

He had got right round his enemy in the darkness and had cut off that enemy's inferior forces from all immediate hope of succour.

It must have been at a great expense of men and of horses that this considerable night march of full twenty miles was undertaken on the top of those two other rapid movements to and from Kenilworth. It was a particularly hazardous experiment which attempted such a feat of physical endurance immediately before what was bound to be a strenuously fought action, although against inferior forces, but it is by taking such hazards that battles are won; and it must be remembered that a great part of the army consisted of men who had not been fatigued by the previous expedition. Indeed, so considerable was the royalist force that it was able not only to cover the direct road to the north by Harvington Hill, but as it would seem the whole line across the loop of the river in which Evesham stands. Simon de Montfort saw them against the morning as they topped the hill and began their advance downward into the Plain of Evesham, and gave that famous cry, "The Lord have mercy on our souls, for our bodies are Prince Edward's."

He prayed in silence at some length, received Communion, and then led his men for the only attempt that was possible for a man caught in such a trap: an attempt to break the line which the enemy had drawn from the river to the river. It was a hopeless attempt even under such a leader. It was foiled, and Simon's command was surrounded: no quarter was given, and it was wholly destroyed.

When this great soldier's horse had been killed under him, and he was still holding his own on foot in the *melée*, he is said to have asked whether his surrender would be accepted and to have had answer that there was no treating with traitors. His son Henry, his heir, fighting at his side, fell first. Simon himself was struck down immediately after.

When the victory was complete, of all the gentlemen-in-arms that had fought under that leader, ten only remained alive—and all those ten were wounded. Even the King (a man never of great strength and now near his sixtieth year), compelled by De Montfort to appear in the ranks of the battle, was nearly struck down in the general slaughter, and saved himself by crying to the man that would attack him: "I am Henry of Winchester, man!" And his son heard him and saved him.

This complete victory ended the third phase of the business and the strategical history of the war. Much separate reduction of rebellious and isolated castles was necessary, notably for the reduction of the Cinque Ports; but after the result of Evesham, the consecutive history of the rebellion and its chances of success are alike ended.

CHAPTER VI
MEDIEVAL WARFARE—III
THE WARS OF THE ROSES

The third great military episode in the English Middle Ages is commonly known as "The Wars of the Roses," because the rival factions between which this civil struggle was waged were headed by the House of Lancaster and the House of York, of which the first took for its badge a red, and the second a white rose.

The period covered extends from the loss of the French provinces by the English Crown to the defeat and death of Richard III, the last of the Yorkists on the field of Bosworth.

The date, therefore, which is the origin of our study, is the return of a certain Lancastrian, the Duke of Somerset, in 1450, from Normandy, which province he had managed to lose for the English King, and which from that year remained a French possession, while the Battle of Bosworth, taking place in 1485, gives us a total interval of thirty-five years for this conflict.

It is not easy to reduce those thirty-five years to any orderly scheme which shall exemplify the principles of strategy. The problem is further complicated on account of the absence of any clear principle whereby we may distinguish between the two factions which alternately rose and fell between the return of Somerset in the middle of the century and the defeat and death of Richard III within fifteen years of its close.

It is difficult, indeed, to describe in ordinary military terms an action which is decided—as were many of the actions in this war—by the sudden treason of one leader, by the unexpected aid given during the very heat of some battle to a Yorkist enemy by a Lancastrian chief, or to a Lancastrian by a Yorkist. The matter is further embroiled by a whole series of incidents comic in their suddenness and lack of reason;

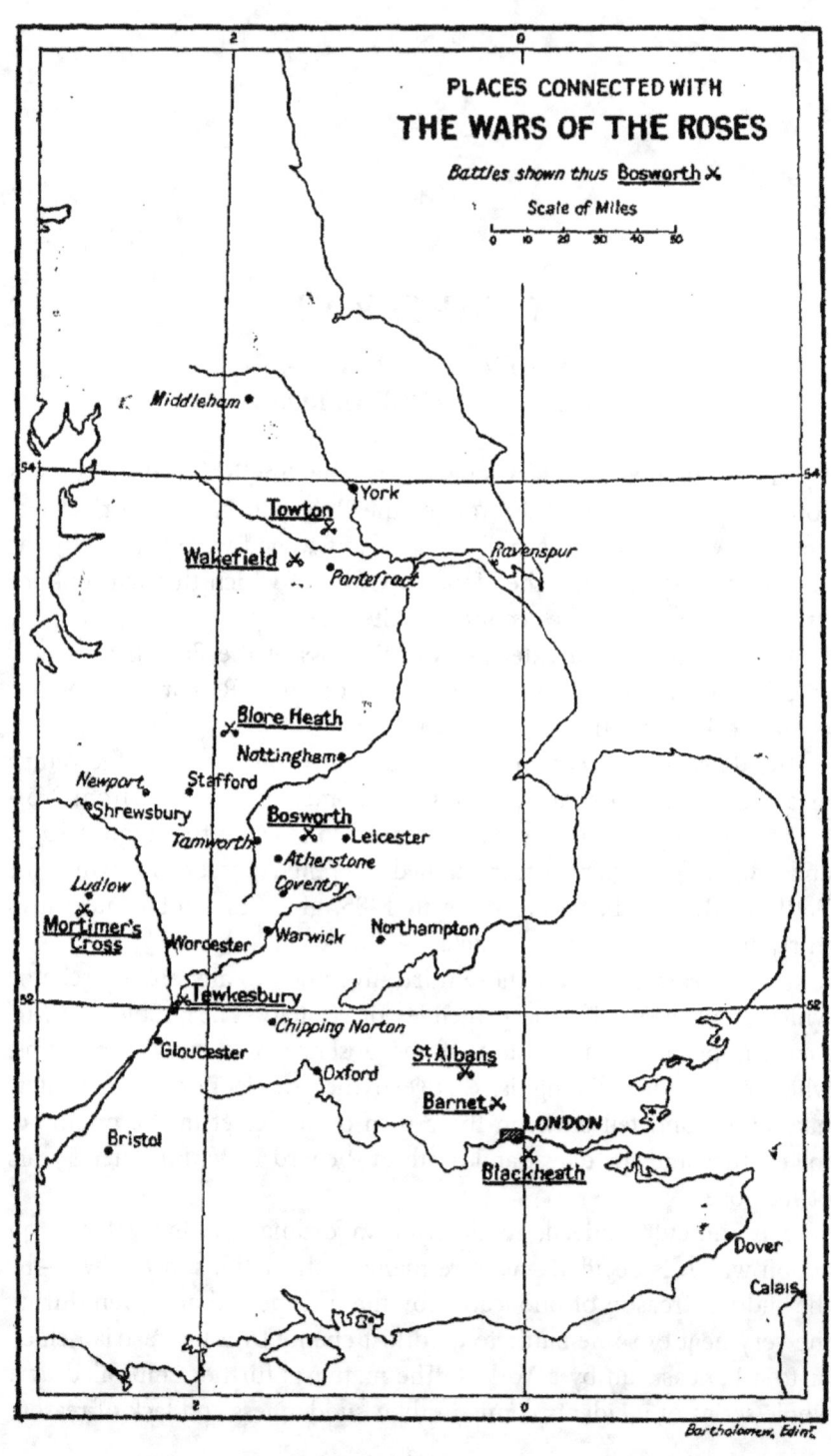

incidents such as the sudden disappearance of a whole army and its refusal, for some political reason, to accept a decisive action; incidents such as the unexpected appearance upon the coast of one or the other party in the guise of the invader coming in too strong a force to be resisted, and the melting away of resistance before him.

The effect of all this apparently meaningless counter-marching, personal betrayals, and the rest, is to leave the student of the period in despair, at least in the earlier part of his study, of disentangling those few main lines upon the fixing of which alone the character of military operations can be comprehended and remembered.

One scheme does solve the problem, and make of this most involved chapter in all the military history of England an understandable and analysable thing. By a proper distinction between certain leading phases, an examination of each phase, of the causes and consequences of the victories gained by either party, we can seize and retain so true a plan of the Wars of the Roses that the innumerable details of that generation can group themselves in due order about it.

Three phases must be clearly seized—

(1) The first extends through nine years: from the moment when King Henry VI first marched against the Duke of York in 1452, to the final victory of the Duke of York's son in 1461 at Towton, and his establishment, for the moment, firmly upon the throne.

The next ten years, 1461 to 1471, must be regarded as an interval dignified by no true campaign and marked only by the suppression of Lancastrian risings.

(2) The second phase of the Wars of the Roses is the short campaign in the spring of 1471 which was decided by the two great battles of Barnet and Tewkesbury, and again confirmed Edward IV upon his throne, after that capital quarrel with Warwick, his chief supporter, which quarrel for a moment had all but undone the King.

Another fourteen years must be regarded as an interval during which no great military operations are to be discovered, full though they are of the threat of hostilities and of perpetual and cruel reprisals falling upon individuals.

(3) The third phase opens in the summer of 1485, when, on the 1st of August, Henry Tudor sails from France to attack Richard III, and concludes three weeks later, when, upon the 22nd of the same month, the invader utterly defeats that king, kills him, puts an end, upon the field of Bosworth, to the whole business of York and Lancaster, estab-

lishes in England for more than a century the dynasty of the Tudors, and closes in this island the book of Medieval History.

Before considering the military details of these three phases, we must first recognise certain political matters which determine the whole period.

When we were speaking of the Campaign of Magna Charta we spoke of an England which enjoyed the full civilisation of the Middle Ages. The central government, that is the King, was far more powerful than any one subject. The *castles*, upon which, ever since the Conquest, the military story of England had turned, were garrisoned of right by royal troops, their commanders, though often hereditary and enjoying a quasi-possession of this or that fortress, openly held of the King and were always revocable by him, not only in legal theory but in social fact.

Even in that second chapter of medieval history, the revolt of De Montfort against Henry III, those old conventions were still secure, and, indeed, it was a proof of the power of the Crown that rebellion against it should have to be upon so formidable a scale and should attract to itself all the grudges and ambitions of a powerful aristocracy and of the great town of London.

But a century and a half after De Montfort's alternate success and defeat, there had occurred in England a revolution of profound effect to all the future history of the country in many ways, and notably in the dislike or incapacity of our people for democratic government. We feel it still. This revolution was the violent usurpation of the crown by Henry of Lancaster, who became, by that action, Henry IV.

The story can be briefly told, and, though it was acted fifty years before the outbreak of the Wars of the Roses, must be told before those wars can be understood.

King Edward III, who reigned throughout the middle of the fourteenth century, from 1327 to 1377, rendered his reign glorious by military successes abroad which, though he outlived their effect, powerfully impressed the people of this country. His son and heir, the Black Prince, the boy of Crécy and the victor of Poitiers, did not survive him. The Black Prince's son came to the throne as a young lad, under the title of Richard II. He reigned for somewhat over twenty years. It was a period of very rapid social change. The French language, once the universal tongue of the noble and military class and of the Court, was being absorbed by England. The great shock of the Black Death had permanently unsettled society, the Feudal system, with its orderly conception of tenure and of mutual rights and duties, had grown old and fantastic, religion was menaced by a new atmosphere of heresy succeeding heresy, very different to the sporadic outbreaks of earlier time. In a word, the Middle Ages had begun to die and their agony was to last a full century.

Perhaps the principal quarrel raised by the dissolution of the old medieval scheme of society was whether its heir in the future should be a strong central government reposing upon the populace, and gradually crushing the great, or a strong aristocracy forming the basis of government at the expense of both the Crown and the people. French development between the Middle Ages and modern times took the first of these two roads. English development took the second: it has ended, as we know, in an England essentially oligarchic, with the central power of the Crown virtually destroyed, and the reins of society in the hands of the wealthy class which was but yesterday an amalgamation of squires and great merchants, and is, to-day, whatever you may choose to call it—a plutocracy or what you will. All this, whether it is good or evil, we largely owe to the action which Henry of Lancaster took when he thrust the rightful Plantagenet King from the throne which had dominated all the English Middle Ages, and occupied that throne himself.

Richard II, as I have said, was the son of the Black Prince, and the Black Prince had been the eldest of the sons of Edward III. Of Edward's many other children four only concern us. Lionel, who came next after the Black Prince; John, called John of Gaunt; the Duke of Lancaster, who came next, and Edmund, Duke of York, who came next again. Such was their order of precedence, and, failing an heir to Richard II, in that order should the male descent of the Crown have gone. The son of John of Gaunt, the first cousin, therefore, of Richard II, Henry of Lancaster, taking advantage of the deep resentment which many of the great nobles felt against the rule of Richard (and also the fact that Richard had no heir), came back from exile in the year 1399, thrust Richard from the; throne, and made himself king under the title of Henry IV, immediately after which usurpation he killed his legitimate rival.

Now it is characteristic of this crime, and of the time in which it was committed, that the usurper could not be secure unless he reposed upon an aristocratic party, and he and his son, Henry V, after him, and the ministers of his grandson, Henry VI, during all the earlier part of that grandson's reign, successively weakened the old religion of royalty in England. They enormously advantaged the squires: they gave these country gentlemen (who then, of course, owned far less land than they do now, for they were then surrounded by a free peasantry) the beginnings of their later power over local government, and inevitably the Lancastrian dynasty, as it was called, could not but permit the wealthiest of the aristocracy to achieve something like independence.

The glorious adventure of Henry V, his conquest of northern France, and the name of Agincourt, masked much of this from the eyes of the nation; but when the child Henry VI, whom he left upon the throne, lost, town by town, the whole of his father's conquest, the change through which England had passed was clearly apparent. The greater nobles were almost independent of the crown, their readiness for revolt was best expressed by Richard, Duke of York, who had, indeed, from his father's side, less title even than the Lancastrian, being descended from that younger son, Edmund, of whom I have spoken: Edmund was his grandfather, but, on his mother's side, he could trace himself indirectly, through yet another maternal ancestor, to Lionel, the eldest son after the Black Prince.

No great heed need be paid to these personal claims of his. The Duke of York fought Henry VI, ultimately supplanted him, and was supported by a considerable body of the great nobles simply as the head of a faction; and the King himself, Henry VI, though enjoying actual kingship at first and the traditional rights of a father and grandfather who had both reigned, was himself little more than the head of an opposing faction calling itself Lancastrian, and hoping, just as its opponents did, for material profit as the result of Civil War.

With these premises we can open the story of the Wars of the Roses in 1450, just half a century after the Lancastrian usurpation had transformed the medieval society of England. We shall find the wars very different from those we have previously examined: castles held by the great nobles virtually as private property; now one king and now another dependent upon the personal service of such men; the motives of action often no more than personal reprisals for personal injuries; and the whole business thick with sudden treasons, changes from side to side, the melting away of great levies whose few lords suddenly refused to support the cause for which they had come into the field; and, in consequence of all these features, a see-saw of power which is not settled until the whole matter is resolved at Bosworth.

The First Phase (1452–1461).

The first phase of the Wars of the Roses is that which begins with the march of Henry VI and his supporters against the Duke of York upon the 16th of February, 1452. It concludes with the great victory won at Towton by the Duke of York's son on March 29th, 1461, and divides itself into *four* clear military episodes which I will separately number.

I

The first of these episodes in its complete futility and odd personal calculations strikes at their very outset the note which was to mark all the Wars of the Roses. But futile as it is and short, certain of the main elements of which is to follow are already apparent, and the first of these is that perpetually recurrent element in English military history, the recruiting power and the differentiation from the south and east of the Welsh marches. It is to the Welsh marches the Duke of York sent his letters asking for a levy wherewith to attack not the Crown but the evil advisers of the Crown, and in particular Somerset, the King's Lancastrian cousin against whom, since his recent loss of Normandy, so large a body of English opinion had arisen. That letter was sent first upon the 3rd of February to the men of Shrewsbury, and in a few days, having gathered an army, the Duke of York, who, as descended from the Mortimers, was powerful in the Severn Valley, marched on London. Henry, accompanied by Somerset, upon the 16th of February, as I have said, went out to meet him, but York had no intention of an action. His intention was much more to throw himself upon his undoubted popularity in London—and what London meant in medieval warfare I have already sufficiently emphasised.

Henry, however, was King. He commanded such regular garrison as London had. York found the gates shut against him. He proceeded south of the city into Kent and, in this same month of February, still had round him something like 17,000 men when he reached Dartford.

York's reason for avoiding the King and slipping south of him, on this eastward march of February 1452, was simple enough: the Royal army was far larger than his own. It followed him up, encamped on

Blackheath, and with the two main forces thus facing each other, each astraddle of the great Roman road from the coast to London and a short day's march apart, the bishops intervened; a truce was arranged and the first military episode of the struggle (if we can call that military in which no military end is served) came to a conclusion. It had lasted less than three weeks.

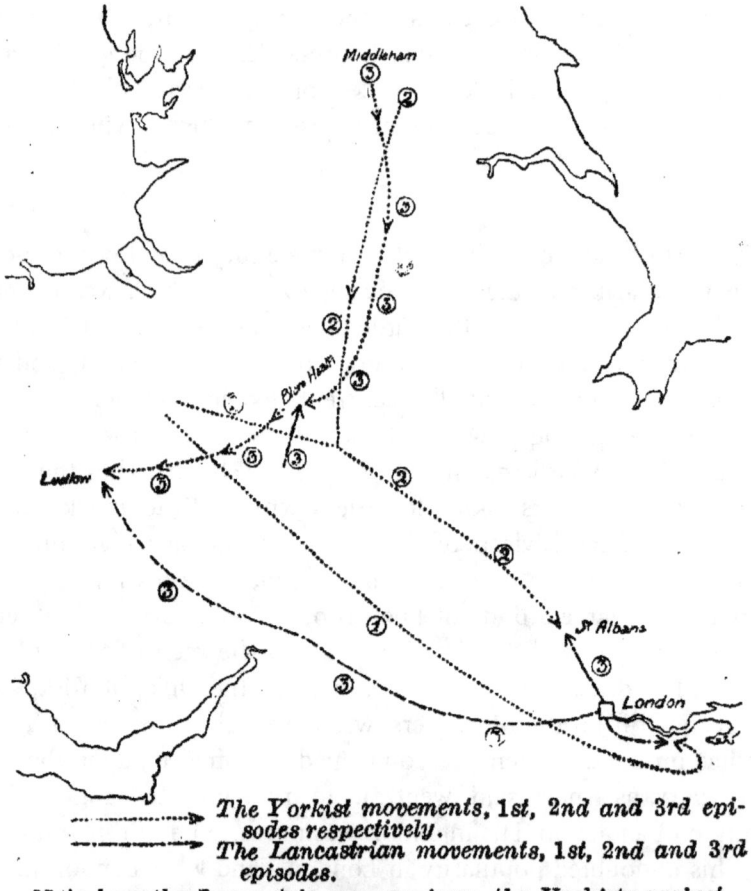

··········▶ *The Yorkist movements, 1st, 2nd and 3rd episodes respectively.*
————▶ *The Lancastrian movements, 1st, 2nd and 3rd episodes.*
Note how the Lancastrians move *from* the Yorkists *against* London.

It is probable that York had expected popular levies to join him from the interior of Kent. Disaffection against the Crown had been so violent in that county as to lead not two years before to Jack Cade's rebellion, but it was probably the very failure and chastisement of that rebellion which prevented Kent from supporting the Duke of York's claims and convinced him of the wisdom of treating. He consented to disband his army on condition that he was allowed to present his grievances (and those, as he claimed, of the whole nation) against Somerset, principally for the loss of France. That first short episode was of no effect military or political, save that York was now the armed leader and acknowledged, of the dissentients, and that the King had proved himself unwilling or incapable of crushing them. It had also this disastrous effect, that to reprieve the prestige of the Lancastrian house an expedition was sent into the south of France, with the sole effect of losing to the English Crown such territories as it still there retained.

II

The second episode of this first phase of the wars was occasioned directly by a calamity which had threatened the Lancastrian party more than once, and which now fell suddenly upon them. The King fell into a sort of paralytic imbecility in the autumn following the last disgraces in France.

Signs of the trouble had appeared in the summer of that year 1453, and as the year proceeded it was evident that Henry VI was no longer competent to govern. He came through his mother of the mad French blood of old King Charles; in body as in mind he had always been weak; and here, now just at the close of his thirty-second year, the inherited curse had fallen upon him.

Almost coincidently with this disaster, upon the 12th of October, 1453, that powerful, brave, unpopular woman, Margaret of Anjou, the Queen, bore Henry an heir to the throne who was to be known under the title of Edward, Prince of Wales. That birth only meant further misfortune. Under the circumstances of his father's health, the legitimacy of the child was doubted among the populace, while to the Duke of York it meant a necessary change of policy. To aspire to the guardianship of a childless King was one thing: with an heir born to the throne and acknowledged by Parliament mere guardianship of the King meant very little. True, the King's breakdown made it necessary to call the Duke of York again into the councils of the Government, but once there the Duke of York's ambition was no longer the control of the Crown, but the Crown itself. His influence in the council was immediate. Somerset was imprisoned at the end of the year; by March, 1454, the peers declared him Protector and Defender of the Realm. He at once filled the great offices of State with his party, put his brother-in-law, Salisbury, into the Chancellorship, and, while he kept Somerset in prison, proceeded to confirm his power on every side. It is important to note that York was practically King of England, though without the title of King, for very nearly two years. It explains his attitude and the support he received in the immediate future.

At the end of 1455, the King recovered his reason, declared the Protectorate of York at an end, and on the 6th of March following gave the governorship of Calais (which York had declared himself the governor of) to Somerset, whom he released. On the 7th he dismissed Salisbury from the Chancellorship, and attempted to reconcile the factions by promising a decision under arbitration.

The Duke of York met this political crisis in military fashion. He at once went north, joining his brother-in-law Salisbury and that brother-in-law's son, his own nephew, Warwick (whom later they called the "king-maker"), levied quite a small force of 3000 or 4000 men, and on the 21st of May, hovering rather more than a day's march north of London with his force, wrote to the King saying that while he was loyal to the Crown he must secure his own safety against Somerset. That letter was probably intercepted. At any rate Henry marched out with a quite insufficient body of some 2000 men up the Edgware Road. Somerset was with him. In a skirmish of perhaps half an hour, York had forced the streets of the little town, killed Somerset and a handful of others, and captured the person of the King himself, whom he found in a tanner's house wounded in the neck by an arrow. After that success York continued his march upon London, bearing the King with him, and after negotiations which do not concern us was again Protector of the Realm, with Salisbury as Chancellor and Warwick as governor of Calais. The importance of that second appointment will soon be seen. So ended the second episode in the first phase of the war.

III

The third phase of the war is like the first, a completely futile series of military operations with no military conclusion. Though York had re-established his power in London he had, now Somerset was dead, no direct complaint to make against a particular evil counsellor. His claim became frankly personal, and aimed at Henry's removal: he was therefore opposed by the energy and determination of the Queen.

The King soon recovered through her ability his full ruling power, but he kept Warwick in Calais, while York remained in London—too powerful for a subject, and particularly for a subject out of office.

The breaking point came in the autumn of 1459. Salisbury gathered 5000 men at Middleham in Wensleydale, just under the Pennines, and started off to march round those hills to the Welsh marches, where York awaited him at Ludlow. Ostensibly that meeting was merely arranged in order that York and Salisbury should present their claims to the King, but Salisbury had an armed force in the field and, though he was not openly marching against the King, the Queen made her husband issue a warrant for his arrest. She gave the dangerous task of executing it to Lord Audley. He intercepted Salisbury's march westward when that commander had just crossed the Dove and was at Blore Heath in Staffordshire. Salisbury defeated and killed Audley on the 23rd of September and made his way to Ludlow. But when Salisbury had there effected his junction with the Duke of York the two, still pretending no more than an interview with the King, found the Royal army not only too strong for them, but attracting to its side certain veterans of the French wars whom the Yorkists had engaged. The King stood with his large force in that bend of the river south of Ludlow which lies between Vinnall Hill and Tinkers Hill. Salisbury and York were within the town itself and round the castle, with Warwick also, Salisbury's son. After the defection of the French veterans they had no choice but to disband their forces and fly, York to Ireland, Salisbury and his son Warwick by sea to Calais. Such was the inglorious and somewhat ludicrous conclusion in the autumn of 1459 of the third episode in the first phase of the war.

The fourth and final episode was to be a very different matter.

IV

Warwick had been permitted to retain commandership of Calais and the command of the fleet until this last quarrel, for it had always been in the mind of the Court to temporise with the Yorkist party. He was now by royal command deprived of both. And Somerset, the son of York's old enemy, was sent to take possession of Calais. Warwick refused to give up the town. Somerset's ships deserted to him; Warwick sailed to Dublin to discuss matters with the Duke of York, came back to Calais, crossed the Channel, landed in Kent with only 1500 men, gathered levies which multiplied that number at least by twenty

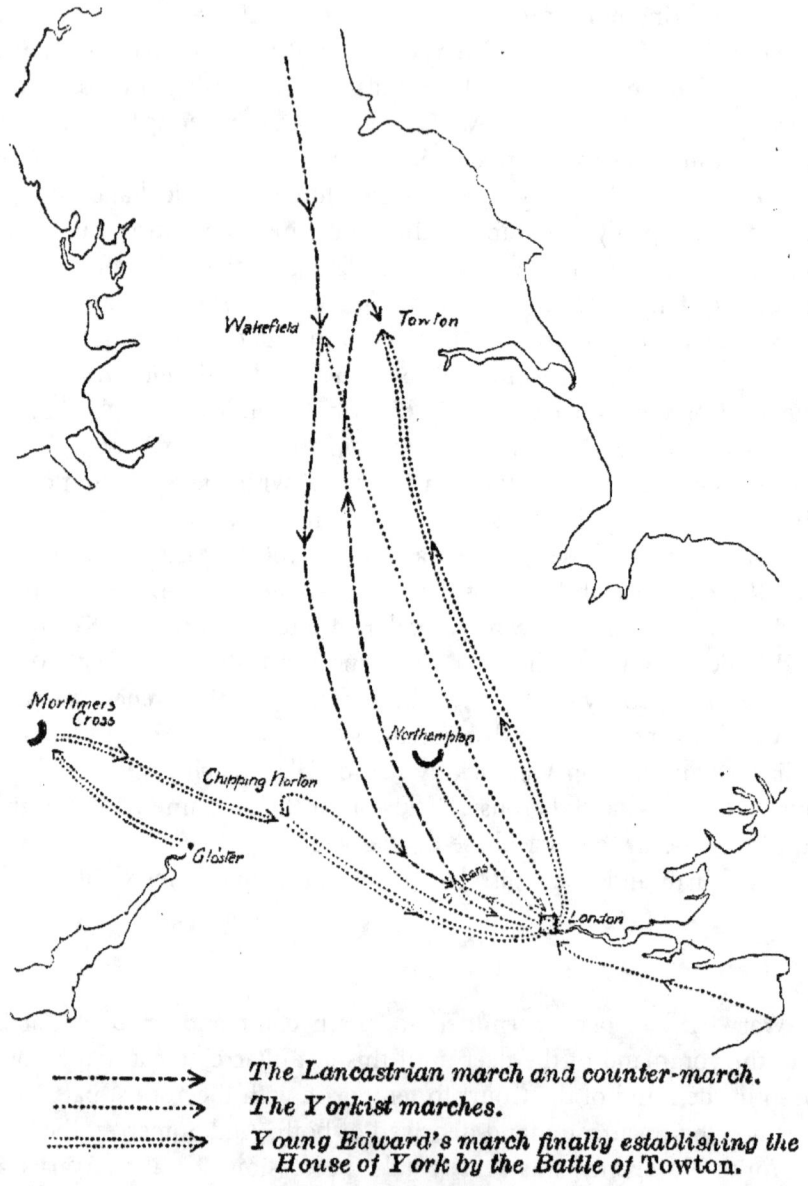

----→ The Lancastrian march and counter-march.
·······→ The Yorkist marches.
:::::::→ Young Edward's march finally establishing the House of York by the Battle of Towton.

THE FOURTH EPISODE

Note how the Yorkists in this last episode depend on London.

and perhaps by thirty, was received very favourably by London, which threw open its gates to him, and promptly marched against the King, who had entrenched himself at Northampton.

It was a swift move. The landing in Kent had been on the 26th of June, 1460, London was occupied exactly a week later, and a first action at Northampton was fought on the 10th of July, a week later again. Warwick and his large force were completely successful. The King was taken and brought back to London by Warwick, the Queen fled to Scotland, the Duke of York returned to London, and at last openly claimed the throne.

But the revolution was too violent to be as yet accepted. A compromise was drawn up on the 25th of October whereby Henry waived the rights of his little son, and permitted York and his heirs to succeed after his death. All that was settled by the end of October. Before the end of December, to be accurate, on the 29th of that month, York, marching north to meet forces which Margaret had raised from her refuge in Scotland, was defeated and killed at Wakefield.

The sequel of this great victory was as curious as it is memorable. It should almost naturally have followed with the Pretender killed, with a Royalist army wholly victorious, that the wars should have come to an end, and should have been decided in favour of Lancaster. The exact contrary happened, because, instead of two regular forces being organised to meet each other, every battle was a shock of loosely coherent levies fighting much more as followers of individual lords who followed an interest, not a cause, than as soldiers of a united force.

Not only York but Salisbury, his brother-in-law, had fallen at Wakefield. Of the trio that had hitherto worked together, Warwick only was left.

In spite of the defeat of the main army under his father and uncle, Warwick set out from London with the King in his custody. And here we must note one element that made for the ultimate triumph of the Yorkists after this discomfiture: they were still the more military body of the two loosely organised opponents. It took the Queen nearly two months to cover the 150 odd miles between Wakefield and St. Albans, a distance easily coverable in a fortnight and, with some need for haste, possible in ten days. Nevertheless, with her enormous superiority of forces she not only beat off Warwick at St. Albans on the 17th of February, but recaptured the King.

Exactly a fortnight before, the Duke of York's son and heir, another

Edward, a boy of twenty, determined to recover even against such odds the terrible blow of Wakefield and his father and his uncle's death. He gathered an army from Gloucester, beat off a local Royalist advance made against him from Wales and defeated it at Mortimer's Cross, marched rapidly across England, met Warwick (who had fallen back after his defeat) at Chipping Norton, and marched with such speed that he held London by the end of the month, while the amazing truth is—possible only to such a war as that of the Roses—that Queen Margaret and King Henry had remained for eleven days within striking distance of the capital without attempting to enter it. They had feared lest their ill-disciplined levies should loot the place and alienate that public feeling which throughout English history made of London so formidable a military factor.

Once the new young Duke of York had London he had everything. Within the week of his arrival he was acknowledged King. Such was the character of the Queen's army that, in spite of its two recent victories, she thought she had no choice but to retreat. Young Edward followed right up England, marching almost as rapidly as Harold had marched, and on the 29th of March he utterly destroyed his enemies two hours south and west of York City on Towton Field. It was an action won by sheer pressure, through a dense snowstorm, for nine hours, from nine in the morning to six in the afternoon, ending in the pushing back of Lancastrians against the River Cock, and a pursuit and slaughter of them in which half of their whole great host perished. Somerset had the luck to ride off to York. He took the King with him, but as a fugitive; and with this decisive action, a Sunday battle, ended the first and by far the most confused phase of the Wars of the Roses.

The remaining two, as we shall see, were brief and clear campaigns.

The Second Phase.

After the decisive action at Towton had made of Edward IV a King and of Henry VI a fugitive, the suppression of anti-Yorkist risings, especially in the north, are the only military incidents in an interval of ten years. Neglecting the political history of that interval, the quarrel with Warwick, much the ablest soldier of his time, with his master and cousin, the temporary imprisonment of Edward and the equally temporary restoration of Henry, the next distinct phase of the Wars of the Roses falls in the year 1471, and maybe called the Campaign of Barnet.

The elements of that campaign were as follows:—

Henry, under the tutelage of Warwick, was nominally the acting king in England. Edward was an exile upon the Continent. In the early part of the year, 1471, Edward raised money privately from his brother-in-law, the Duke of Burgundy, and with a fleet of eighteen vessels which can have conveyed but a very small force* he sailed from Flushing. He made right across for the Suffolk coast, but the vessels were seen. He feared opposition and sailed northward, putting at last, under stress of weather, into the Humber. He landed where Henry of Lancaster had landed more than eighty years before, at Ravenspur, now under water, just inside Spurn Head, in the mouth of the Humber, on the 14th of March, 1471, and marched to York under the pretence that he merely came to claim his estates, while he gave orders to his little force to cheer for King Henry. On the day when he reached and rested at York, he still acknowledged Henry's sovereignty and the right of the Prince of Wales to inherit.

He set out from York for the south.

There is, as the reader will remember from the introductory chapter of this brief survey of our military topography, a strategical point of capital importance in the line of advance from the north upon London. This strategical point is Pontefract. We saw it to be important because its situation and stronghold commanded the passage of the River Aire. Both the Roman road to York which bridges that obstacle at Castleford and the alternative and parallel road somewhat to the east, which crosses it at Ferrybridge, are commanded by any force that may be lying at Pontefract. It is an hour's march to the one crossing and half an hour's to the other, while both can be simultaneously watched by any force holding the castle and the town, as we have previously seen.

Moreover, as we have also seen, the obstacle of the Aire here blocks the narrowest passage between the Pennines and the Fens. At Pontefract, two days' march south of York, lay Montague with a force that could not only have prevented Edward's further progress south, but could have destroyed his little army.

Edward crossed the river not four miles from the position of that hostile command, marched south right across its front, and no opposition was offered him! He made along the great London road due

---

* He is credited at the most with 1500.

south for Nottingham, and in the fifty odd miles' marching, now at last through country that was more favourable to his cause, he gathered one contingent after another until, upon reaching Nottingham itself, he found himself at the head of 7000 men, and at last declared himself King.

Now in all this there is no element of strategy. The invader comes with a handful of men, receives at first no recruitment, marches

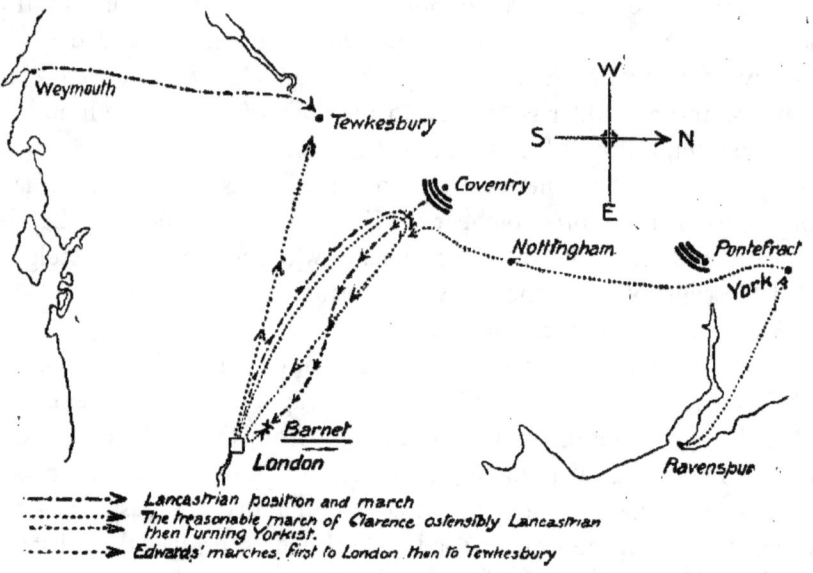

THE SECOND PHASE OF THE WAR OF THE ROSES Barnet & Tewkesbury.

through a country upon the whole hostile to his claims, and the obvious solution of such a position would be the fixing of that small force by whatever large levies the forces of the Crown could gather, and its destruction.

Nothing of the kind was attempted. No force at all, large or small, blocked York's little command, and in its progress southward he is allowed to pass Pontefract, as we have seen, to increase his force, and to reach Nottingham; and this absurdly unmilitary situation must be explained, like so many of the grotesque anomalies of these wars, in a manner purely political and personal.

The explanation is this. When Warwick had quarrelled with Edward IV, driven him out and restored Henry, Edward's own brother, the Duke of Clarence, had been involved in the quarrel and had suffered as a partisan of Warwick's. He still publicly counted as Warwick's ally and Henry's, but secretly he had determined to return to his brother's allegiance—and Edward knew it. With a commission from Henry, Clarence had raised a considerable force. That force was marching up from the south, ostensibly in Henry's cause, to join Warwick near Coventry. Clarence had urged Warwick, and through him the other Royalist commands that might have blocked Edward's progress, to do nothing until he, Clarence, should have arrived with his great reinforcement.

Here, then, were three bodies all converging upon the neighbourhood of Coventry: (1) Warwick's command which already lay in that neighbourhood; (2) Edward's 7000 hostile to it, which was approaching from Nottingham and the north; (3) Clarence's, the largest force, nominally marching up from the south to effect a junction with Warwick, but really designing to effect a junction with Edward, his enemy. Warwick, still trusting in Clarence's good faith, remained in the neighbourhood of Coventry, and allowed Edward to pass in front of him unmolested; Clarence effected his junction with Edward, and this double force of the Yorkists lay next day at the town of Warwick, between Coventry and London, and with nothing to prevent Edward's final marches upon the capital.

To gain London now, as always through the Middle Ages, was to gain the chief military asset in the kingdom. Edward entered the city with a very large force now under his orders, upon the 11th of April, Maundy Thursday. Undoubtedly the populace was Yorkist, but apart from that certain of the great political officers in the city had taken up Edward's cause.

Insufficient though his forces were, Warwick marched south at once when he saw how Clarence had betrayed him. Edward spent Good Friday in London. On the morrow, Saturday, he proceeded out of London one day's march by the alternative road to St. Albans, having King Henry with him as prisoner. Warwick had advanced with such speed that he had passed St. Albans already; and on Easter Sunday, April 14, exactly a month after Edward's landing in York, the shock between the two armies took place near Chipping Barnet. Warwick's command was destroyed, and Warwick himself killed. It was this action at Barnet which was the single decisive blow of this short campaign, on which account it should bear the title of that battle.

Edward had indeed two other difficulties to deal with, but they were easily surmounted.

On that same Easter Sunday, Henry's Queen had landed at Weymouth with the Prince of Wales. Her force, though large, hardly merited the name of an army, so loose was it. Edward, marching west, at once intercepted it at Tewkesbury, and destroyed it in its turn by a victory in which the Prince of Wales, among others, was killed. This success was won upon the 4th of May. Upon the 5th, a cousin of Warwick's, still in command of a fleet, landed in Kent with a considerable force and marched on London. He was refused an entry, passed up west to intercept the return of Edward from the Severn Valley, but whether from a promise of personal pardon, or disheartened by the news of Tewkesbury which had just reached him, he abandoned his command; and on the 21st of May Edward re-entered London at the head of 30,000 men, and the second phase in the Wars of the Roses was closed. The same night in the Tower, the pawn of all these years of fighting, Henry VI, may have been murdered, and certainly died.

The Third Phase.

The third and last phase of the Wars of the Roses is even briefer and more decisive than the second. For fourteen years the House of York had been secure. Upon Edward IV's death his brother Richard usurped the throne. At the head of those who still maintained the Lancastrian claim was a young man of twenty-seven, one Henry Tudor, who from his exile first in Brittany, then at the Court of France, still planned the overthrow of the reigning house. His claim to the throne was absurd, or rather non-existent. He was descended from a line of Welsh squires on his father's side, and though on his mother's he could trace his descent from John of Gaunt it was by a branch at once illegitimate and specifically barred from inheritance. But while his claim by any theory of medieval kingship was negligible, his moral right to lead the continued protest against the House of York was very strong, for his father, Jasper Tudor, who had been made Earl of Richmond, was half-brother to Henry VI, the son by her second marriage of that French princess whom Henry V had married to complete his conquest of France. In social fact, if not in feudal theory, he had lived the life and occupied the position of nephew to Henry VI; and all the forces of rebellion and discontent, to which upon the close of those fourteen years the supposed or real crimes of Richard III added increasing weight, would follow Henry when he should attempt the throne, more loyally and more cohesively than the Lancastrians had yet been followed. The campaign in which Henry established himself upon the throne of England, and closed at once the Wars of the Roses and of medieval warfare in England, is much the simplest and most direct sort to follow, and occupied but three weeks from beginning to end.

It was upon the 1st of August, 1485, that Henry sailed from Harfleur in the mouth of the Seine, a port of good augury to one who bore the name and continued the tradition of the victor of Agincourt. He had with him but 3000 men, very few of them English, most of them Norman.

Richard III was an excellent soldier. He organised a system of intelligence far superior to any that the Wars of the Roses had yet seen, with posts of cavalry dotted along the south to warn him of the approach of his enemy or of his return, and he at once dispatched

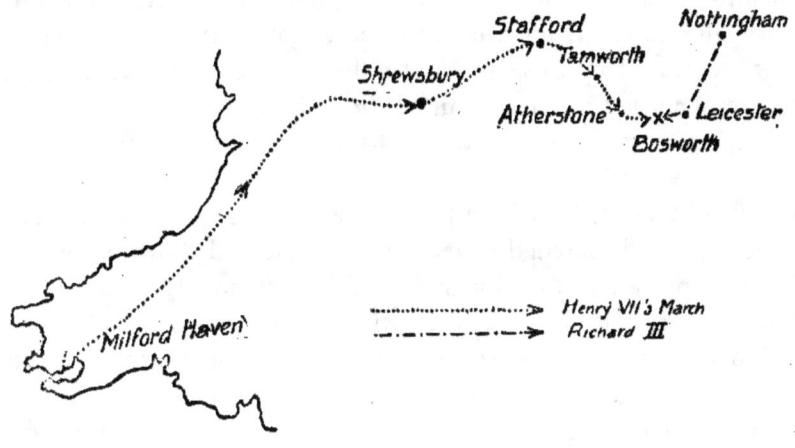

THIRD PHASE OF THE WAR OF THE ROSES

a fleet to intercept that enemy in the Channel. Henry's fleet slipped past the ships that were looking for it, cruised for six days in the light weather round the longships and across the mouth of the Bristol Channel, and it was not until Sunday, the 7th of August, that the small but well organised command disembarked at Milford Haven.

At this point it is essential to consider yet another of those personal factors which are so important throughout the whole length of these conflicts, from the first claims of the Duke of York, thirty-five years before, to this last and successful assault upon the throne.

A man powerful as a leader and commanding considerable resources of men and fortune, Lord Stanley had married young Henry's mother, who was a widow. His brother, Sir William Stanley, had the command of the forces in Wales. It is part of the complexity of the situation that both these men were high in the service of Richard III, but their connection with the invader through the marriage of his mother caused Richard an anxiety for which he has been blamed, but which, in the event, proved justified. It was increased when Lord Stanley, a little before the invasion of his stepson, asked leave to visit his estates in Cheshire and in Lancashire. Richard consented to his withdrawal from Court for that moment, but retained his son, Lord Strange, as a sort of hostage against his good behaviour.

It was the action which Stanley took in the events immediately following the invasion that determined the results of it. The moment Richard heard of Henry's landing (which was not until a week after it had happened), he sent at once for Stanley, but Stanley replied that he was ill and could not come. Richard, more certain than ever that he was betrayed by this, his chief military subordinate, caused Lord Strange, who had in part admitted the treason, to write to his father and urge him to come and join the King if he wished to save his son's life.

Having done this, Richard gathered a well disciplined and considerable force and marched for Nottingham. He had shown at once his soldierly aptitude in thus making for the Midlands. He was in a post of observation, as it were, from which, with a disaffected country behind him and the consequent difficulty of organising his intelligence, he could watch the advance of the invader from whatever quarter it might proceed. He was also in a central position upon which the levies that he had summoned might most quickly converge from the extremities of the island; and Northampton from York and beyond, Norfolk from East Anglia, Howard from the south joined him with their several levies.

Meanwhile, the invader Henry had marched up from Milford to North Wales. William Stanley had joined him with his command. He debouched from the mountains on to the plains of the Upper Severn, crossed that river at Shrewsbury, and struck straight for the Midlands where Richard was awaiting him. Two days' marches on, at Newport, on the boundary of Staffordshire, Talbot joined him with a levy of his tenantry. At Stafford, the end of the third day's march in the open country, Henry made his private agreement with the Stanleys. In order to save the life of Lord Strange, the hostage, Stanley's command should not actually join his own, but should retire before it as though intending to join Richard as it had been summoned to do, but that retirement was to be a feint only. At this moment, four days before the shock, the two armies at Nottingham and Stafford respectively, lay about forty miles apart. Richard marched down southward to Leicester, a matter of two days, Henry bending somewhat to the south in his turn (the news of Richard's southern march having reached him at least a day after it took place), pressed forward, and in two days was at Tamworth, just off the Watling Street. He reached that town upon Sunday, the 21st of August. During that same Sunday, Richard marched out west from Leicester, covered a normal day's progress of twelve miles, and encamped a couple of miles south of Market Bosworth, just outside and to the west of the village of Sutton Cheney. In camp he lay that night with his army, but during that same night Henry marched along the Watling Street through Atherstone, where the Stanleys joined him, and then, by what is left of a Roman side way from the Watling Street to Leicester, he made in the early hours of the day a trifle north of east for Richard's position, two hours' march from Atherstone.

Under any circumstances but those which characterised the whole of these wars, the victory, when the shock came upon that morning, Monday, the 22nd of August, 1485, must have lain with Richard. He was nominally at the head of a command twice that of his opponent in numbers. He was certainly the better soldier. He had established among the men immediately under his order the better discipline. But the now apparent treason of the Stanleys, who were advancing to the field joined to the invader, and, what was perhaps more grave, the deliberate inaction of the northern contingent under Northumberland, outweighed the King's advantage. More than this, there was in the situation an element which counted very strongly in any medieval army consisting of separate levies, and that was the personal disaffection of many of the men and their leaders. In the result, therefore, Richard's forces, such as still held to him throughout the struggle, were scattered, and Richard himself, in the thick of the press, fighting with a conspicuous courage and crying, "Treason! Treason! Treason!" went down.

The victor had accomplished all this so early that he could ride into Leicester in triumph that same night; and the Wars of the Roses were done. There was no further struggle upon any scale worthy of strategical analysis and record between great armed bodies within the borders of England until the Civil Wars of the seventeenth century.

CHAPTER VII
THE CIVIL WARS

Because they were the last piece of regular warfare waged within the borders of England proper, and because they had so momentous an effect upon English society, destroying the old popular centralised monarchy and replacing it by an aristocratic system, the Civil Wars take on, in the eyes of Englishmen, a military importance at which foreigners are apt to smile.

In other words, their political meaning to us is so great that it exaggerates for us their value as a military exercise.

The numbers engaged upon either side of the struggle were usually small. Skirmishes outside country houses are dignified by the name of sieges; a melee of a few horse is often called a battle, while the lack of plan and purpose in much of the fighting makes the general observer underrate, if anything, the position of this English episode in the general military history of the seventeenth century. He thinks of it as a sort of isolated and petty event thrown up by the general commotion of the Thirty Years' War and of the vaster struggle which was proceeding throughout Europe between central authority and the oligarchic principle of government.

Small, however, as were the numbers engaged, and amateurish and sporadic as was the strategy displayed, the military side of the Civil Wars must be grasped by any one who desires to understand the history of England. In their main lines they illustrate, better than any of the fighting since the Norman invasion, the general strategical conditions of English topography, and they developed a really great cavalry commander, Cromwell,* whose name counts high among European

---

* I would not fall into the pedantry of calling him "Williams," though this was of course his real name, and it was as Oliver Williams that he signed that financial document to which he attached most importance.

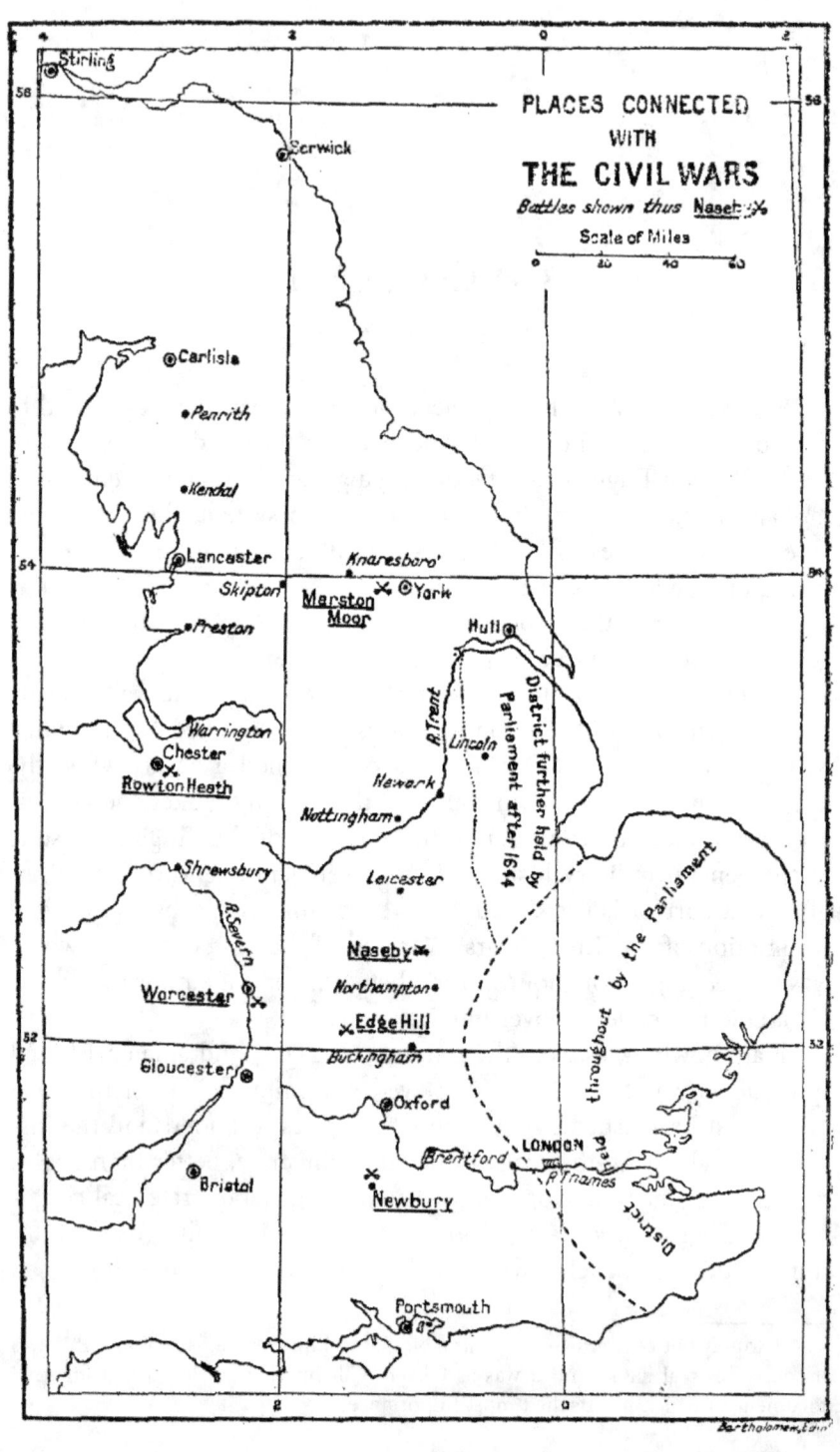

statesmen of the time, and to whose initiative can be traced not a few of the commercial developments which England enjoyed after his time.

In order to grasp the strategy of the Civil Wars (which at first sight appear to be no more than a confused welter of marching and counter-marching across the face of England), we must clearly seize that factor which has been so often insisted upon in this book: the special military position of London.

I will not here recapitulate the many points which the reader will find in the passage I have devoted to this subject. It is enough to recall to him what the preponderance of London was in any great struggle fought upon English soil, in what way it served as a depot, recruiting base, financial resource, nodal point, and obstacle.

Now London (probably most of its populace and certainly its great merchants and those directing the organised life of the capital) was for the Parliament. It not only overshadowed and (as it were) contained Westminster, it also furnished the revenue upon which the Parliament could levy troops. It furnished in the earlier part of the war a considerable proportion of the recruitment, it served as a permanent base whence armies could proceed and to which they could retire, and it commanded the crossing of the Thames up to sixty miles from the sea; it prevented any combined action upon the north and south of that river for some miles eastward of its own longitude.

This last point is of capital importance and determines the whole scheme of the Civil Wars. Parliament was supported by London, by Kent, and by East Anglia.

Was there any similar geographical area that could be counted on the side of the King? There was not. Upon the whole the Severn Valley and the northern counties contained, among the wealthier classes, a larger proportion of Royalists than the rest, but with the exception of the undoubted solidarity against the King of London, and of the squires and merchants of Essex, Cambridge, Huntingdon, Norfolk, Suffolk, and Kent, it is difficult to establish a geographical basis for the fighting that was to follow.

The name Cromwell had been affected by his family for some years as adding social distinction to the gigantic wealth which gave the Williams' their position in the Eastern Counties. It was as the cadet of this huge fortune accumulated from the spoils of the Church that Oliver Cromwell was introduced to his great career in which we must never forget that he made another fortune by combining military with commercial enterprises.

On the other hand, the very fact that London and the eastern counties thus held together "polarized" the war—if I may use that metaphor. The very fact that Charles could not attempt London and the east compelled him to rely upon the west. The west was not wholly his by any means; at the very beginning of the wars we have Worcester, cutting the Severn Valley right in two, garrisoned by the Parliament: at its critical turning-point Gloucester on the same side is decisive.

Any one making a map of the places both defensible and open which, in the first months of the war, were gainsaid by Royalist or Parliamentary forces, and marking the one in red and the other in blue, would find that he had a parti-coloured pattern everywhere save in London and the adherent counties which I have mentioned; but he would find the King's colour predominating on the Upper Thames, upon either bank of the Severn and north of Trent.

The most general formula, therefore, with which we can cover the story of the English Civil Wars is that they consisted upon the whole in a recovery by Parliament, reposing upon London and the east, of the west and north in so far as the west and north had been the King's.

The Civil War develops from that moment on January 10, 1642, when King Charles left London for York. There is a preliminary period during which the two parties each hesitates to engage and each "feels" the situation. The first military incident in which the right of the Crown to command all stores, armed forces, etc., was questioned was the refusal of Sir John Hotham to deliver the magazine at Hull into the King's hands. This refusal took place on the 23rd of April. By June Englishmen had everywhere before them the curious spectacle of a double recruitment proceeding in nearly every county; for the Parliament under an *Ordinance of Militia*, issued, of course, without the King's consent; for the King under a *Commission of Array*, which was a royal order.

The first actual blow struck was in connection with the fortified town of Portsmouth, where Goring was in command. Upon receiving orders from the Parliament he returned, after some hesitation, the answer that his allegiance was one directly to the King, and he preferred an oath to his troops upon the lines of that declaration. Whereupon a siege was immediately laid to the town by those forces which admitted the authority of Parliament.

But all these incidents were but the preliminaries to the formal opening of the war; and the date from which that must be counted is August the 22nd of this same year, 1642, when King Charles, with ritual solemnity, summoning "All those north of Trent and twenty miles south of that river," ordered the ceremony of the "Raising of the Standard" to take place in a large field outside the town of Nottingham where he lay.

Two thousand men surrounded the colours; 4000 more at the most completed the little force. Against these 6000 the recruitment of the Parliament had aimed at a total number of 16,000 for its side. The total forces which it had actually enrolled and armed by this date, August the 22nd, was somewhat more, and Essex, the principal Parliamentary General, lay at Northampton with his command alone numbering 15,000 men.

There was one last attempt made upon the initiative of Charles, after this formal "Raising of the Standard," to prevent Civil War. The Parliament refused his advances, and regular hostilities began.

The Civil War lasted as a whole just over nine years.

Its first date is this 22nd of August, 1642. Its last, the defeat of young Charles II at Worcester on the 3rd of September, 1651.

It falls into three clearly marked divisions—

(*a*) The first is of not quite two years, is indecisive, though upon the whole favourable to the King; but it ends disastrously for him in the battle of *Marston Moor* upon the *2nd of July*, 1644.

This battle of Marston Moor is the true turning-point of the war.

It is followed by the re-modelling of the Parliamentary Army.

(*b*) The second phase then opens and ends somewhat two years after the first phase with the capture of Oxford on the 20th of June, 1646.

The capture of Oxford came at the end of a number of Parliamentary successes of which the greatest was the central victory of Naseby, exactly a year before. The fall of Oxford was but the last of a long series of efforts in which Parliament had gradually worn down the King during this second phase of two years, and had taken nearly all his garrisons and had defeated all his armies in the field. It appears to close the whole story.

There is no more regular warfare between the King and Parliament (I omit and refer to its proper place the conflict with the Scotch), but five years later the short third phase of the war consists in (*c*) the unexpected march of Charles II, now lawful king after his father's execution, into Lancashire and down the west of England. This phase may be said to begin with Charles's leading his 11,000 (or 14,000) men out of Stirling on the 31st of July, 1651, and to end thirty-five days later with his total defeat at Worcester upon the 3rd of September.

These three phases cover the whole of the struggle.

THE FIRST PHASE.

The first phase of the Civil Wars is clearly divided into (1) a preliminary episode, which is best remembered by the name of *Edge Hill*, and (2) a series of isolated actions which cover the year 1643, which continually increase the power of the Royalists but which lead up in 1644 to the active aid lent by the Scotch to the Parliament, and the final blow at Marston Moor.

(1) I have said that Charles at Nottingham, upon the 22nd of August, 1642, commanded but 6000 men. Three or four days south of him at Northampton, and covering London from any attempted advance on the part of the King, lay Essex with 15,000.

Such an advance was, of course, out of the question with the King's small force. What Charles very wisely did was to retire westward up the valley of the Trent, and by way of Stafford upon Shrewsbury. By the time he had reached that town and recruited men not only upon the march but in the town, he was at the head of nearer twenty than eighteen thousand men, and with this force he proposed to march upon London.

Here let the reader note once again what London means in the military topography of England. Charles might march upon the City: he could not count on taking it, and all those characters which I have so continually emphasised, and which have saved London from siege or even from pillage through so many centuries, made it certain that the Royal Army could not attempt its reduction and might fail in attempting even its occupation.

Charles's advance none the less struck London with panic and confused the plans of Parliament. Had it come to an actual assault or to trying to hold down that vast population with such a force as Charles commanded, the Civil Wars would have ended far earlier than they did and would have been equally disastrous to the King. We shall see how, as a fact, Charles was compelled to hesitate before the Capital, and in the end to withdraw.

When Essex knew that Charles had undertaken his march westward towards the Severn Valley he made all speed to march westward himself. He aimed at Worcester where the Severn is nearest to the Midlands and to Northampton, and he garrisoned that town, thereby cutting the Severn Valley. But he soon discovered that Charles's object was not a defensive occupation and garrisoning of the Severn line, but an advance on London.

The Parliamentary General received the most urgent orders to counter-march and intercept Charles if it were possible by coming in between him and the Capital. In this Essex failed, but he pursued the King rapidly, and, on the 22nd of October, came into contact with

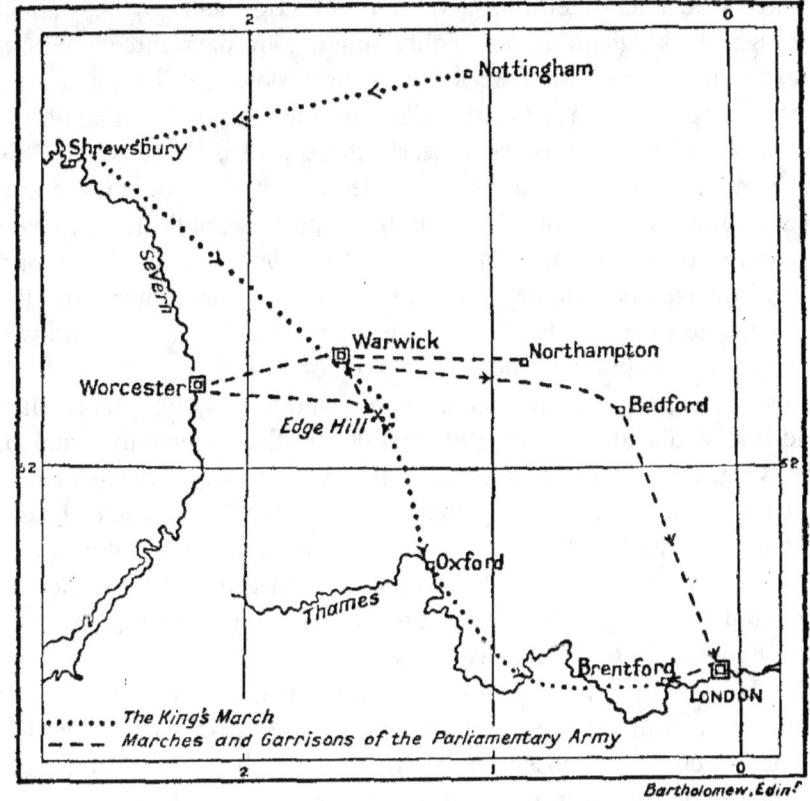

his enemy at Kineton, a short day's march out of Stratford upon the London road from Worcester. The Royal Army had ended their day's march on the far side of Edge Hill, which lies at about an hour's march in front of Kineton. They turned back to meet Essex, and on the following day, October 23rd, was fought the *Battle of Edge Hill*.

It was a very confused and uncertain business. The numerical superiority* of the Royal Army and their further superiority of position (they occupied the northern slope of the hill) should have secured them the victory. It was, perhaps, the imprudence of Rupert's Cavalry in too prolonged a pursuit and pillage which rendered the result tactically indecisive. Essex was free after the action to withdraw his forces upon Warwick, a day's march away. Charles enjoyed the immediate strategical result of a victory, for he was able to pursue his march unmolested; but his failure to destroy Essex was to cost him dear.

Few things in the Civil War are more remarkable, and few were more disastrous in their consequences, than the sluggishness of Charles's advance after this action. From Edge Hill to the Capital through Buckingham is not eighty miles, four days forced marching; five long days, and a week for the very slowest calculation, even with a large force. Yet Charles did not find himself in the neighbourhood of London for very nearly three weeks. He took the little Parliamentary garrison at Banbury, delayed at Oxford, hung about near Reading for no conceivable military purpose, and did not begin to approach toward the neighbourhood of London until the second week in November. He had given Essex time to come down from the Midlands to the Capital; Windsor was held by the Parliament, and two further posts between Windsor and London.

Even so the Parliament came very near to making peace. They had miscalculated the strength of opinion in the country in favour of the King, and his march disturbed them. They negotiated with him at Colnbrook as he came up the western road. By a breach of faith upon their part Brentford was occupied during the negotiations; and Charles, indignant at this sharp practice, charged and took the village and the bridge with fifteen pieces of artillery and five hundred prisoners. But though he was at the very gates he could do nothing with London. The mere numerical power of the levies which Essex opposed to him, bad material though they were, made that certain. Some 24,000 men opposed the Royal Army for the whole of one critical day upon Turnham Green. Charles turned back through Reading

---

* Charles's command seems to have been superior to the total of Essex in any case, but when we consider that Essex had wasted men in garrisoning Warwick and Coventryas well as Worcester, and that, even of his marching column, a quarter under John Hampden was too far in the rear to come into action, the great superiority of Charles in the field is certain.

to Oxford, which City is henceforward the pivot of the Royalist action throughout the rest of the War.

So ended what I have called the episode of Edge Hill, which had been the first phase of the struggle. What we have next to follow and what forms the close of that first phase is far less clearly marked.

There was, of course, sporadic and isolated fighting all over Engand,* but the map of this struggle can be best seized if we consider three main areas.

(1) The Royal Army at Oxford, which from Oxford as a centre raids, captures, garrisons as best it can. It has opposed to it, throughout the whole spring and summer of 1643, the inactive command of Essex lying on the Chilterns and in the plain to the west and at the foot of those hills.

(2) An army in the north under Newcastle, which had for its business the conquest of Yorkshire, and ultimately a convergence upon Oxford and a junction with the King.

(3) An army in the west under Prince Maurice and Hopton, whose business it was to advance eastward and northward, increasing the area fully controlled by the Royalists and ultimately also converging upon Oxford.

When this convergence from the north and from the west upon Oxford should have been effected, what with the much larger contingents Charles would then command and the successive defeats and loss of public position upon the part of a Parliament, Charles calculated that he could safely march on London, which would then receive him.

Keeping this clear plan in mind it is easy to co-ordinate the triple accidents which befell each part of the triple scheme.

The western force was opposed in the main by Waller as Parliamentary General. Strategically it was successful. By the 5th of July the head of the Royalist advance was at Bath, and inflicted a heavy defeat upon Waller; while, in an attempt to contain Hopton a week later in Devizes, Waller suffered the descent of Wilmot, who had marched from Oxford, and the Parliamentary Army in that quarter was wiped out. Bristol fell to Prince Rupert exactly a fortnight later; and one may

---

* If the reader wishes to acquaint himself with the enormous mass of record and the utter confusion of the time, let him turn to the scholarly book called The Civil War in Dorset, by Mr. A. C. Bayley, and he will sufficiently understand the difficulty of disentangling even the main lines of the conflict.

say that with the end of July 1643 the plan had succeeded so far as the junction of the western army with the central army at Oxford was concerned, and the general occupation of the west by Royalist forces.

But the reader must note one important exception which turned the scale: *Gloucester was still garrisoned by a Parliamentary force.*

Turning now to the north, we find Royalist successes there which are at first almost equivalent to that in the west. The Parliamentary General opposed to Newcastle was Fairfax. Newcastle advanced, establishing Royalist posts in nearly the whole of Yorkshire, and pushing back Fairfax into the corner between the Humber and the sea, whose capital and military depot is Hull. But the northern successes, though considerable, were not complete. The line of communications between Oxford and the north was kept up through *Newark*, which was garrisoned for the King, but the country in between was in no way held. And that for this reason: Lincolnshire was got hold of by the local Parliamentary bodies and added to that belt of eastern land which was solid for the Parliament; and here it was the genius of Cromwell as a leader, coupled with the prestige surrounding the immense wealth of the family from which he sprang, which was chiefly responsible for the success.

A glance at the map will show how Lincolnshire, held upon the flank of the narrow gap between the Yorkshire plain and the hills, would prevent any secure communication between the Midlands, with Oxford on their south, and that Yorkshire plain, even had it been fully subdued by Newcastle. But it was not fully subdued. The successes of the Parliament in Lincolnshire permitted Fairfax to rally, and by the autumn of 1643 all that can be said of the Royal successes in the north was that they held their own not quite up to the line of the Humber.

Now, in reviewing the general situation of the summer of 1643, what you get is this: the west has been upon the whole thoroughly recaptured for the King and the western army has effected its junction with the Oxford command, but to this apparently complete success there are two very important modifications. First, of the total forces levied in the west many had refused to proceed to the Midlands and to abandon the neighbourhood of their homes—the junction with the Oxford command, therefore, though strategically effected, did not mean, as it should have meant, a large numerical increase. Secondly, one important garrison still held out for the Parliament—the garrison of Gloucester. Meanwhile, the northern successes are not complete,

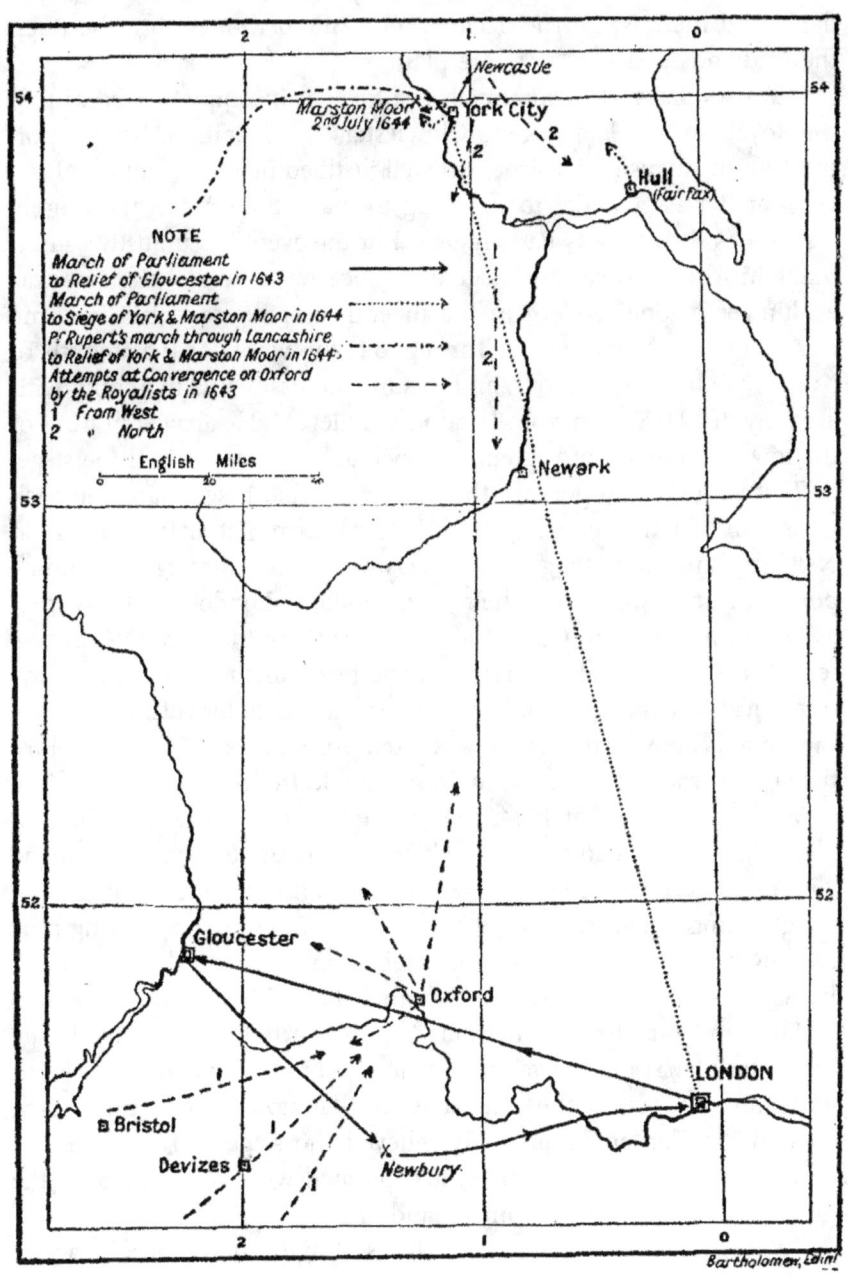

and though communications are open between Gloucester and the north by way of Newark, they are badly threatened on their eastern flank, and there is no true occupation of the belt of country between the Midlands and the Yorkshire plain.

It was under such a combination of as yet incomplete success that the Royalist Army laid siege to Gloucester. The operations began upon the 10th of August. This siege was well justified by the condition of the war, for it was essential to the King to make the west as thoroughly his own as the east was Parliament's. But the event has unjustly caused many historians to call the siege of Gloucester a blunder. If there was a blunder it appeared not in the inception of the task, but in some miscalculation of its gravity. Throughout the whole of that month of August Gloucester held out; and meanwhile Essex was marching with an army of 12,000 men from London to relieve it. He arrived in front of the town on the 5th of September, revictualled it, and raised the siege.

That is the capital point of the year 1643. That Essex marching back upon London happened upon the Royal Army (itself in retreat) at Newbury, and there fought an indecisive action is strategically unimportant. Fairfax went on, as he had intended, to London; and the King, as *he* had intended, to Oxford. But the raising of the siege of Gloucester left a Parliamentary garrison in the heart of the west, proved the numerical weakness of the King's command, and, by cutting through the united line which Charles was attempting to form from Yorkshire through Newark and Oxford to Somerset, destroyed that combination.

With the opening of 1644, everything began to change. In the first place, Parliament had made an alliance with the Scotch, and on the 25th of January the Scotch crossed the Border. In the second place, the King, calling a halt to a struggle in Ireland which had been long proceeding between Royal forces and a rebellion, summoned his troops in Ireland to come over and join him in Britain. Five regiments landed in Flint and marched upon Nantwich, where there was a small Parliamentary garrison; Fairfax was ordered across England from South Yorkshire, and upon the same day as that upon which the Scotch crossed the Border, he not only relieved the siege of Nantwich, but destroyed, captured, or actually incorporated with his own troops the newly arrived regiments from Ireland.

This double date, January 25, 1644, is of high importance. It meant, in the first place, that there was no possibility of junction between Newcastle and Yorkshire and the King in the Midlands and the west—

since Fairfax had marched in between with impunity and struck his blow right across the line. It meant, in the second place, that the Royal forces in Yorkshire were now between two fires: the Scotch on the north, the Parliament on the south. Rupert in the spring, by a series of excellent cavalry actions, did recover Cheshire and South Lancashire. Further, he had prevented the Parliament from capturing Newark, to which they had laid siege. But for all these successes (which extended the Royalist area into the northwest, and maintained at Newark a point which might prove useful in the future if Yorkshire should have been but held), the great plan of the year before had obviously fallen through. There had been no general concentration at Oxford. Even the west was not completely held, for Gloucester still held out. The Royalist force in the north had failed to effect its junction with Oxford, and was now itself in peril.

Newcastle, on the arrival of the Scotch, had thrown himself into the town from which he took his title; the Scotch had besieged him for three weeks without avail. They abandoned the siege to march southward. Newcastle followed them; but the new combination of the Scotch forces with the pressure exercisable by the Fairfaxes to the south of him compelled him to throw himself into York. When the Parliament sent up Manchester with 14,000 more men, Newcastle saw that the fate of the north would be decided within the next few days. He sent urgently to the King in Oxford for succour. But the Oxford command was itself in danger, and was too small to break through into the north. It had enough to do to elude the Parliamentary armies, and to save its 7000 men by marching and counter-marching between the Midlands and the Severn Valley.

Rupert still remained, however; he could be sent from his successes in Lancashire to the aid of Newcastle, and he received orders from the King to march at once upon York, effect his junction with Newcastle, raise the siege of York and save the north. He immediately obeyed. He crossed the Pennines in the last week of June, 1644. On the 27th of that month his advance guard was at Skipton, with York but forty miles away. On the 28th his main body was on the saddle of the Pennines. Upon Sunday the 30th, the Parliamentary Army under Cromwell and Manchester, besieging Newcastle in York, heard that Rupert was already at Knaresborough, only one long day's march away. They raised the siege, and on Monday, the 1st of July, Rupert marched into York city and effected his junction with Newcastle.

This was the critical moment of the whole war. Two considerable forces lay within striking distance of each other. Rupert and Newcastle, now combined and at the head of more than 23,000 but less than 25,000 men, had immediately to their east an enemy's force of at least equal magnitude, which had retired from before the walls of the city a distance of five miles. The situation called for a decision, and the victory of either party would determine the whole fate of the north. If the Royalists should be the victors, that would make possible a march south and a junction with the King in the Midlands; if they should be defeated, that would destroy the northern army as a factor in the war, isolate the King, and leave him certainly doomed to see his inferior forces worn out and destroyed.

It was upon the morrow, Tuesday, the 2nd of July that the united forces of Rupert and Newcastle marched out of York city eastwards to meet the enemy. They came upon him at Marston Moor between Long Marston and the River Nidd. All afternoon the two forces watched each other without an engagement. Rupert depended upon a ditch which ran across the field for sufficient cover, and awaited the attack. Six o'clock passed and the attack was not delivered. The Royalists did not believe it would be delivered that day. Rupert upon the left wing dismounted (as did some of his officers), and called for supper. Immediately, though the sun was already near setting, the right wing of the Parliamentary Army cavalry, which Oliver Cromwell commanded, charged. The various fortunes of the two lines, the defeat of Rupert's horse, the converse defeat of the Scotch and most of the Parliamentary infantry, the recovery of the situation by Cromwell's return from pursuing Rupert and his charging of the successful Royalist Infantry in flank, made up the three tactical phases of the battle. It was the last, Cromwell's second charge, which decided it completely in favour of the Parliament. Fifteen hundred prisoners and every Royalist gun were by sunset in the hands of the rebellion; and with the fall of darkness upon that Tuesday the issue of the war was really decided.

The Second Phase.

I trust I have made clear the main strategic lines of the first phase in the Civil Wars, and the two principal incidents which, in determining that first phase, determined also ultimately the whole fortunes of the struggle.

It had been intended for the army of the south-west to occupy everything for the King over that region and up to the Midlands, making for Oxford as the rallying point. It was further intended for the army in the north under Newcastle to occupy all the open land north of Trent until this spreading area of occupation should also join up with Oxford. Meanwhile at Oxford, the King's headquarters, the third army should have its centre and raid outwards towards the other two, and in general, confirm that policy of occupying the whole west of England, which was the prime strategic purpose of the King.

The relief of Gloucester, coupled with the failure of many of the western levies to leave their homes, destroyed the first, or western, part of this plan. The second, or northern, had been even less successful; it was in particular threatened by the advance of the Scotch in aid of the Parliament, when, with the battle of Marston Moor, it was utterly defeated and the north was lost for ever to the Royal cause.

As a result of that disaster, Charles's forces were now strategically confined, so far as their main cohesive bodies went, to the west alone. In the autumn of 1644, and so early as the 1st of September, an astonishing and inexplicable march of Essex's right into Cornwall (which made him suspected of treason) ended in complete disaster; but no such accidental success could retrieve the chances of the King. Nor could the fact that seven weeks later the mass of the Parliamentary forces (with Cromwell amongst them) failed to crush the King at Newbury, upon October the 22nd, where this second battle in the neighbourhood of that town was as indecisive as the first.

But these two checks (for strategically the defeat in Cornwall was as negative as the lack of success at Newbury) brought a great decision upon that man on the Parliamentary side who had the most soldierly eye. This man was, of course, Cromwell. After sundry political moves, which do not concern the general military plan of the struggle, he founded a true standing army to which was given the name of "The New Model." About 21,000 men, very highly paid but subject to a strict discipline, were incorporated. Of this force, roughly one-third consisted of cavalry, two-thirds of infantry.

The motion to create this regular and novel army originated on the 23rd of November, 1644. The ordinance was issued and proclaimed throughout London on the 15th of February, 1645.

Marston Moor had made it certain that Charles must be ultimately worn down. The ordinance of the 15th of February, 1645, made it certain that the business would be quickly dispatched. It was upon the 30th of April that the "New Model," as it was called, took the field.

They were bidden march upon Taunton and afterwards to besiege Oxford, although the unexpected victories of the King's ally or lieutenant in Scotland, Montrose, were already causing anxiety. Charles had marched northward through the Midlands upon the news of those Scotch successes of his party; he took Leicester upon his way, and Fairfax, at the head of the "New Model," was, luckily for him, ordered by the Parliament to pursue.

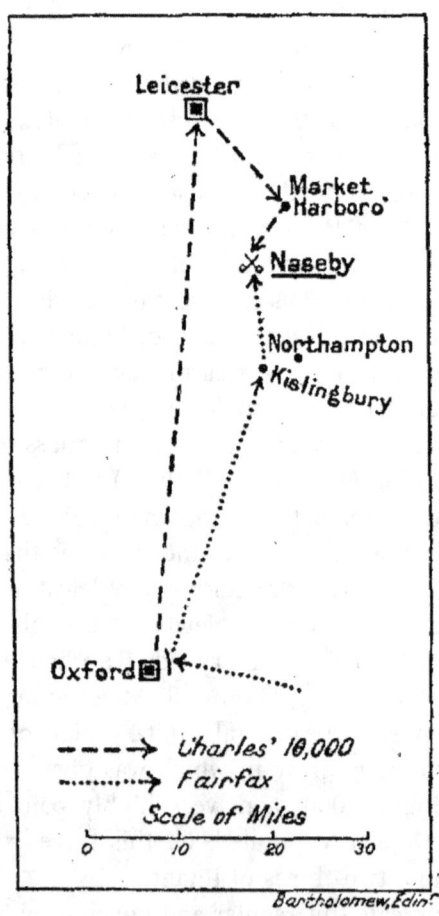

It must carefully be noted that Charles had with him but 10,000 men; as I say, he was being worn down. Of that 10,000 men half were cavalry. They took Leicester by assault, small as their force was, and they committed the imprudence of leaving a garrison in Leicester, reducing their numbers to perhaps little more than 7000, and certainly not more than 8000. Fairfax, who was pursuing fast, was close at the King's heels. Charles turned eastwards and southwards with a very bad intelligence service, and not appreciating his danger. At supper on the 13th of June, 1645, he recorded his intention of marching the next morning up northwards through Melton to Belvoir. That same evening Cromwell, for whose leadership the Parliamentary cavalry longed, joined the army at Kislingbury on the River Nene, three miles east of Northampton. Upon the next day, the 14th of June, the whole army was concentrated at Naseby, three hours to the north, and there awaited the attack of the Royal Army which lay in front of Market Harborough. Why superior forces should have awaited the attack of inferior no modern military historian can explain; the Parliamentary forces were nearly two to one. But at any rate it was Charles who attacked, Rupert, a point of scarlet on his great horse, leading the first charge, and as all the world knows the result was a decisive victory for the Parliament. Again, as at Marston Moor, every piece fell into the hands of the victors, all the King's baggage, and for that matter great bodies of his men as well. The only thing that can be said about this second and crushing decisive victory of the Civil Wars is that, with the numerical superiority of two to one, it is amazing that it was not better managed, for there were moments during its development in which, incredible as it sounds to modern ears, Charles had a chance of success.

Among other things in this defeat, the King's private papers fell into the hands of the victors.

After that blow, the war smoulders out in a series of capitulations upon the part of those scattered garrisons whereby the Royal generals had held so much of England. The King himself went to Wales. The siege of Taunton was raised, Bridgewater was stormed; even Bristol, with Prince Rupert to defend it, fell. His last external army, that of Montrose in Scotland, was fatally defeated upon the 12th of September—a mere remnant, and Charles, standing at last in Chester, saw his own last force defeated on Rowton Heath, as he watched from the city walls. This was upon the 23rd of September, and the war was over. The rest of the conflict is purely political, save for that unexpected march which his young son made five years later, a brief adventure which ended in the disaster of Worcester, and which I have called the third phase.

The Third Phase (*the Campaign of Worcester*).

The third phase of the Civil Wars is a short campaign, which terminated in the Battle of Worcester, and which forms the last military action permanently establishing the power of Cromwell.

The march which Cromwell made against the Scotch, his victory at Dunbar and what he believed to be his consequent immunity from further opposition, belong to warfare in Scotland, and must be dealt with very briefly where I attempt to analyse the main lines of the various Scotch expeditions. It must be enough to say here that he had thoroughly succeeded by the spring of 1651 in occupying the greater part of the Lowlands. He was in possession of Edinburgh, and though suffering from illness in the earlier part of the year, and even proposing a return to England, he was so far recovered by the earlier part of July that he was ready to attempt the line of the Forth which was held against him by his enemies. He forced that line, and Fifeshire fell into his power. Perth surrendered upon the 2nd of August, but in the very moment when he achieved that success Cromwell received the news of Charles's move to the south.

Charles II, the young King whose fortunes in England seemed ruined by the execution of his father two years before, had by that very account found himself able to rely upon the national feeling of Scotland. He had landed in that country and it was round his person that the resistance to Cromwell gathered. He lay at Stirling, which was as yet untaken, when Cromwell succeeded in forcing the line of the Lower Forth and in subduing the north-eastern Lowlands. From Stirling the young man designed that fine adventurous plan which ended in disaster. And, upon the last day of July, while his enemies were thus occupied upon his left, Charles II marshalled his army upon the fields below Stirling Rock and set out for the south.

He marched, of course, by the difficult western road, since Cromwell was in possession of the way along the east, and through Berwick, which was the normal avenue of approach from Scotland to England.

It was a force of something between 11,000 and 14,000 men which began the dash southward: largely composed of Highland elements, and therefore not only lacking the regular discipline which the troops of the seventeenth century had learnt throughout Europe, but also (as is affirmed by those best capable of judging) unfitted to receive such a discipline, they had for their advantage a great enthusiasm, and as they

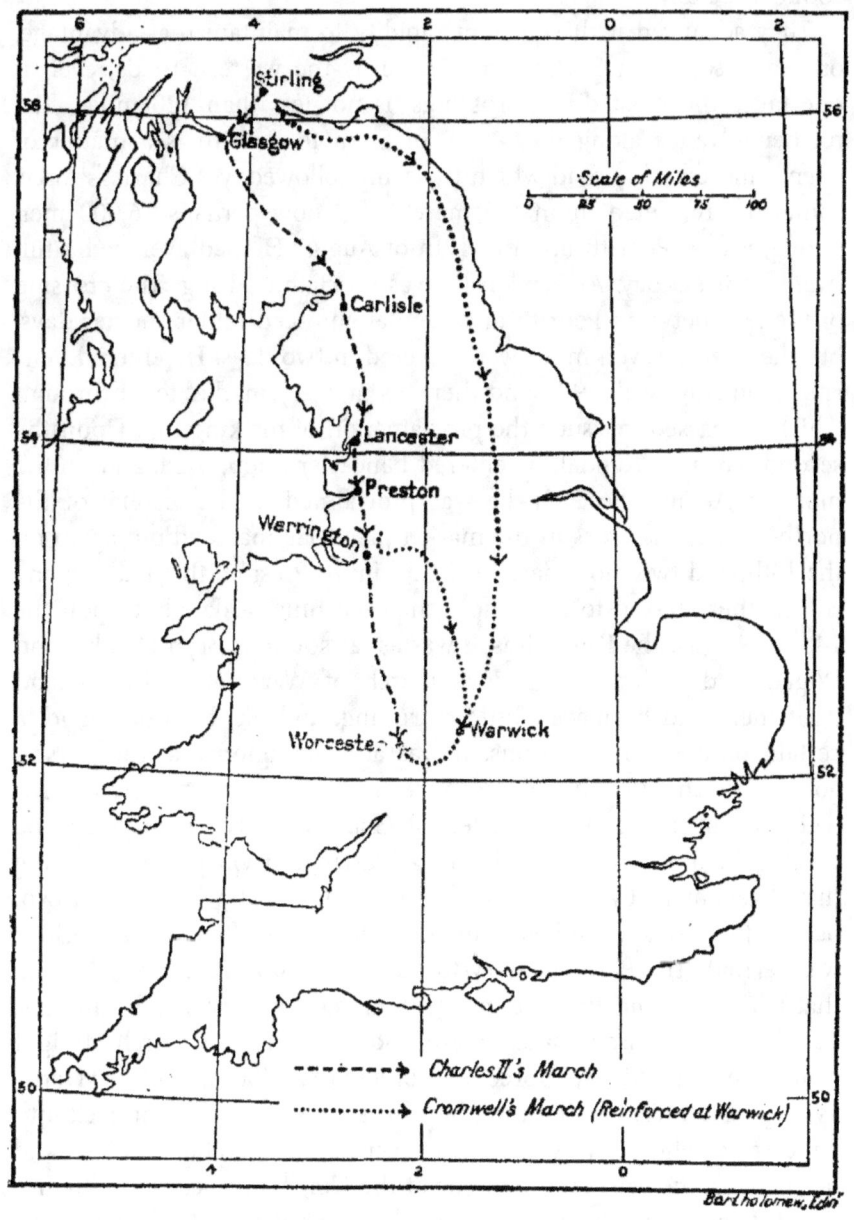

unfortunately for themselves believed, a general backing in England.

The rapid movement gave to Charles II's force an advantage of about three days.

They advanced with sufficient rapidity to maintain that advantage, or nearly so. From Stirling to Carlisle by the western roads, even if one takes the most direct crossings, is not less than 120 miles. The further advance along the Valley of Eden to Penrith is a matter of twenty more by the road which the army followed, yet Charles's force, somewhat recruited upon the march, and now perhaps 16,000 men strong, was at Penrith upon the 7th of August He had averaged a full twenty miles a day. At Penrith he was proclaimed King. The crossing of the fells between Penrith and Kendal enforced rather shorter days, but the twenty-seven miles were covered in two days. He entered Penrith upon August the 9th, and there, as in every market town through which he passed, reissued the proclamation of his kingship. Upon the second day after Kendal, he entered Lancaster unopposed, and on the morrow, August the 12th, he was proclaimed in that capital of the north-west at the cross in the market place. He marched out again on the 13th, and two more days brought him to Preston, the march being still further relaxed to little more than ten miles a day; but upon the 14th of August the King himself was as far south as Bryn Hall beyond Wigan, and within half a day's march of Warrington. In England itself there had been very little recruiting, and on the other hand, a certain number of desertions. It was at Warrington that the pursuit got into touch with Charles's advance. The Parliamentary forces which had been hurrying along the left of Charles's march managed to be a detachment in front of it, holding Warrington village and covering that detachment by another force to the north of Warrington town, but the town was taken before midday, and in the afternoon the bridge was carried. The Parliamentary force retired upon Knutsford, hoping that Charles would turn to engage, tempted by their small numbers; but the enemy disappointed them and continued to march straight south. He received a reinforcement of less than 400 men under Derby as he passed through Cheshire, but this small force was sent back into Lancashire, where it was decided to recruit considerable numbers and to maintain the war upon the rear of the King's advance. That attempt failed. Lancashire did not rise, and the attempt to hold the southern part of the county for the King was broken a week later at Wigton. Meanwhile, six days after crossing the Mersey Charles had reached

Worcester, a very rapid piece of marching again involving nearly twenty miles a day, if we reckon the check in time produced by the fighting at Warrington bridge, and the fact that the forces entered Worcester town, not at the end of a long march, but in the course of a day's advance. With the entry of Charles's men into the town of Worcester, the strategics of the campaign come to an end. Charles fortified the place. Cromwell with the Parliamentary Army reached Evesham four days later, and was virtually in touch with his enemy.*

The numbers of the two opponents were as four to seven, and Cromwell had against a no longer confident and loosely organised enemy of 16,000 at the most, 28,000 men well disciplined and ready for the action that followed. It was fought upon the 3rd of September. It resulted in the total destruction of Charles's army, and the final establishment not only of Cromwell over the Government of England, but of a unity of command and authority from the Grampians to the Channel.

---

* The two places are, as we saw in discussing the campaign of De Montfort, just one fair day's march.

CHAPTER VIII
THE SCOTCH WARS

The warfare levied by English rulers against Scotland and Wales may be summed up thus as to its strategical character: Against Wales the whole action consisted of isolated border fighting from stations or castles in the vales, and particularly where the vales open out upon the Welsh marches, and that border fighting was directed against the hill country. To this general formula, which covers the whole story between the end of the Imperial rule in Britain and the sixteenth century, there is but one exception—to wit, the organised occupation of *all* the castles by Edward I. These combats carry no strategical plan and cannot therefore be summarised here.

As to the warfare of English armies directed against Scotland, if we neglect the promiscuous combats of the Border chieftains it may in its turn be summed up in a simple formula. An English army marches north by the easiest road of invasion, that along the eastern coast: it makes for *Stirling*, the nodal point of the south: or a Scotch army marches south by the same road. An action, usually decisive, is fought to the advantage of one or the other adversary. It fails to decide the campaign; even if adverse the independence of Scotland from England (in a military sense) is preserved.

To this use of the Eastern Road there is no true exception. Every march of consequence, whether Edward I's or Edward II's, or that of the Earl of Surrey under Henry VIII, or that of King James opposing him, or that of Cromwell in 1650, is so undertaken. This applies even to the march upon Flodden, for though the Tweed was crossed upon that occasion a day's march up from Berwick, that exception but proves the rule in this sense: that no army in all those centuries attempted to negotiate the formidable obstacle of the Border hills. It is possible that in the last years of Edward I we should have had a break in so general a sequence of military history, for Edward had summoned his last invading army at Carlisle, but he died before that army could march, and though his heir received Scotch allegiance at Dumfries, upon that western road which with such difficulty outflanks the Border hills of Liddesdale and Cheviot, of Annandale and of Esk, yet there was not at the moment a prosecution of the invasion by so difficult a path; and when, in 1314, the effort was renewed, it was undertaken by the regular eastern road through Berwick. It is true that Charles II, in that wonderful march to Worcester, used the western road, passing through Carlisle and Lancashire, and in the "'15" the Border was actually crossed to the west, while the subsequent march of the Scotch invaders in English territory was towards Penrith and Lancashire; the same is true of the invasion of "'45."

But in regular military operations between each nation before the union no considerable military operation affecting the history of the two countries in any final manner has attempted to pass the wild and deserted Border country save by the traditional eastern road. This is the first and main feature of the warfare between Scotland and England.

The second is that every single invasion which permits an English force (before the union of the two Crowns) to penetrate into the Lowlands between the Clyde and the Forth, is checked sooner or later (and usually sooner than later) by the wall of the Highlands; and sometimes a day's march or so before breaking itself against that wall.

After the legal union of the two Crowns in the junction of the sixteenth and seventeenth centuries (a union purely political and not arrived at by warfare), the problem changes somewhat because the garrisons north of the Border are legitimately commanded by a Government residing to the south of it, and any military action necessarily takes the form of a local rebellion. Even so, the main lines I have laid down remain true, and the Highlands never form a seat of war, not even in the "'45" in any true sense. They have been conquered and transformed in our own day by influences very different from those used by soldiers.

Excluding the seizure of the Scotch Lowlands by Edward I, and King John's raid nearly a century later, three definite campaigns mark regular conflict between the Scotch and the English governments or nations. That of Bannockburn, that of Flodden, and that of Dunbar.

The strategy of each is so simple that their main lines may be laid down very briefly.

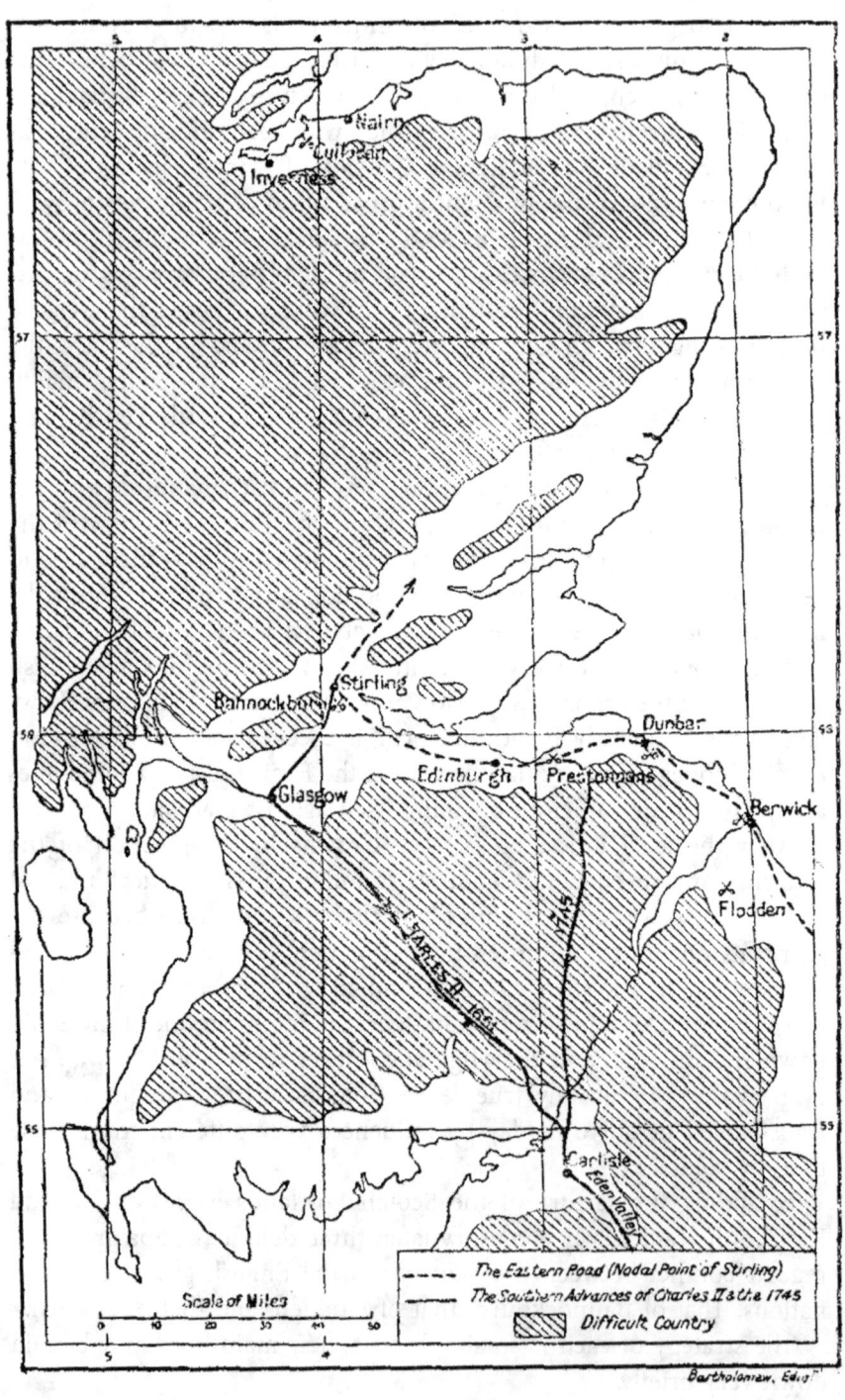

A fourth expedition, not so much concerned with the national struggle as with a sectional one, and concerned with the crushing of the Rebellion in 1745, completes the list.

The campaign of Bannockburn, which was the end of all medieval attempts to unite the two Crowns, was as brief as its strategy was simple. Edward II summoned a force at Berwick to recover the castles and posts which his father had held, but which a national uprising had either taken or imperilled. The object of the march was Stirling, which lies just at the apex of that Lowland triangle which is the best crossing of the Lower Forth, which is the nodal point where the roads to the north-eastern and the western Lowlands cross, and which has, therefore, always been the objective of a march from the south. How large a force met the King at Berwick we cannot tell. It was certainly considerable, if we may judge from the impression produced upon contemporaries, but it was less large than Edward had hoped for, for the opposition that was ultimately to ruin him had already grown strong. Edward left Berwick in the middle of June 1314. He allowed a week for the march to Stirling, he arrived under the rock of that citadel upon the 23rd. The exact disposition of the armies has been and remains a matter for debate, but the best opinion seems to be that the 30,000 or the 40,000 men of the national forces under Bruce lay much along the line of the present road from Stirling to Wallstale, with their right upon the stream called the Bannockburn, and their left in the neighbourhood of Stirling itself. The battle, which resulted in the complete defeat of Edward and his much larger forces, was fought upon the next day, the 24th of June, 1314, and has one principal meaning in the general history of European warfare, which is this: That, for the first time since the Romans, infantry standing unshaken proved that they could resist cavalry, however heavy the shock. It was a lesson learnt and developed throughout the fourteenth century. It decided Crécy, and in the long process of two hundred years changed the art of war. The retreat or rout followed the road by which the advance had been made, and Edward's first breathing space was at Dunbar.

The second campaign, that of Flodden, is equally simple, though its result was the exact reverse. Its date is almost exactly two hundred years after that of Bannockburn, the decisive action being fought upon the 9th of September, 1513.

The advance in this campaign was on the part of the Scotch. Their King, James the Sixth, crossed the Tweed before the English force under Surrey had marched from Pontefract. Surrey commanded perhaps 26,000 men; how many marched under James's command we do not accurately know, but it was certainly 40,000, and very probably more. The result is the more surprising, especially as even the 26,000 which Surrey marshalled were largely composed of hurried levies from the gentry upon the Border. The Scotch marching along the south of the Tweed crossed the Till at Ford (where they destroyed the castle), and went up to that height called Flodden Edge, immediately to the west of the river, which is the last northern outpost of Cheviot. It was a strong position, and again we must note the anomaly that the Scotch, in spite of their superiority of numbers, should have stood upon the defensive. At least the position they had taken up on the height was a defensive one until they found that Surrey had outflanked them. That commander had gone up the right bank of the Till, crossing it at Twizell Mill about a mile from its junction with the Tweed, and so marched from the north against the Scotch, cutting them off from their own country and threatening their retreat. Under that threat, the Scotch force came down northward from the height, advanced to the attack of their inferior enemy, down the hill called Branxton Hill and across the open fields which lie to the south of Branxton village. The issue was not joined until nearly five in the evening: it was decided within an hour, and by sunset the Scotch force was destroyed. Its park of artillery, splendid for the time and consisting in seventeen of the latest pieces, 6000 horses captured and some 10,000 of the enemy slain, was the immediate result of the day, in which not only the King of Scotland himself fell, but from which the power of Scotland never completely recovered.

The third campaign, that of Cromwell, was similarly decided in favour of the southern forces, and after a campaign which followed, as had every important movement into the north for over 1500 years, the eastern road.

It was on the 22nd of July, 1650, that Cromwell crossed the Tweed with 16,000 men. He passed through a wasted country to the very neighbourhood of Edinburgh. He was compelled to fall back from lack of supplies, when he found his retreat barred upon the English side of Dunbar at the point where the Broxburn crosses the Berwick Road. At least, the Scotch force lying upon the heights above this road marched down to attempt its blockade. It was before sunrise that they made this movement. It was not completed when the Scotch discovered that Cromwell had crossed the Burn in the night, and was turning their attempt to occupy the road. The action that followed in the first hours of the day, the 3rd of September, 1650, was so complete a destruction of the Scotch army as to put the Lowlands for the moment at the mercy of Cromwell. He took all their artillery, their colours, 10,000 prisoners, marched back to Edinburgh, received the surrender of its castle before the end of the month, and had nothing left against him that winter but the force at Stirling, from which point, however, in the succeeding summer of 1651 began the fine march southward of Charles II, which ended so disastrously at Worcester, and which I have described in another place.

Of the two rebellions, the 1715 and the 1745, the first resulted in an invasion of north England by a small Highland force which, though it did not cross the western hills of the Border as Charles had done a lifetime before, actually came into England by the west, following to the north of the Cheviot and crossing the Border just north of Carlisle. The little army marched south into Lancashire, was caught and surrendered at Preston.

The 1745 was a far more serious business. In the first place, it began with victories. Upon the 21st of September Prince Charles's army, which already had possession of Edinburgh, broke the first English force sent against it, and broke it in the first few moments of a successful charge. This was at Preston Pans upon the coast, two hours' march east of the capital. The subsequent advance into England followed much the same line that the 1715 had followed, but with a larger though not considerable force. It numbered perhaps 6000 men, and did not cross the Border until so late a date as the 8th of December. This little army took Carlisle, managed to march right down the northwestern road through Lancashire, got past the command which the Duke of Cumberland was leading against it; it had nothing between it and London save the camp at Finchley, and it might hope to count upon the apathy at least of the southern English Midlands and even of the capital. But upon getting as far south as Derby, the lack of any positive support from the districts through which it marched, the difficulty of keeping the Highlanders together, and the fear of the much larger body of the enemy, which they indeed received and outflanked, but which if it should come up to them would certainly prove their superior, made a retreat probably necessary and certainly advisable. The Duke of Cumberland followed that retreat (which was northward by the western road along which the advance had come), but never managed, so rapid was it, to hold the enemy upon this side of the Border. Indeed, in a skirmish near Penrith, his own force was checked by their rear-guard, and, on the fifty-sixth day after they had started out, the Scotch army at the very end of the year reached Glasgow. They were now recruited by further levies, including certain French contingents. They beat off the first English force (which found them at the siege of Stirling) on Falkirk Moor on the 17th of January, 1746; but this was in the absence of Cumberland, a really able man though a Hanoverian, and one who could boast that his recent defeat at Fontenoy had but deservedly increased his reputation as a general, and especially as a leader. Meanwhile, Charles failed before Stirling and retreated upon Inverness. Cumberland, taking command of the royal army, pursued, and though Inverness had fallen to Charles, that Pretender's diminishing force could not expect to meet what Cumberland was bringing against it. Cumberland entered Nairn upon the 14th of April. Charles was persuaded to stand (in spite of his grave inferiority) in front of Inverness astraddle the Nairn road, upon the field of Culloden Moor, and there his force of not more than 5000 men was destroyed upon Wednesday, April 16th, 1746. The most complex, as the most doubtful, of the principal campaigns involving the two countries was in that action decided.

No decision by armed forces has since that day been attempted within this island.

NOTE ON BOOKS

It is impossible to make a satisfactory bibliography of the subject for the general reader, so scattered are the materials for the elementary history of *Warfare in England*, and even the elements of any particular campaign. The first volume of Fortescue's *History of the Army* and Oman's *Art of War in the Middle Ages* expand certain points made in the preceding chapters.

There are various sectional histories of the Civil War—Godwin's *Civil War in Hampshire*, Bayley's *Civil War in Dorset*, and Broxap's *Civil War in Lancashire*, Kingston's books on *East Anglia and Hertfordshire* at the same time, and Money's work on the Battles of Newbury. Of text-books on English military history there are none, except Fortescue's volume, which has very little to do with English fighting, and is mainly concerned with Continental campaigns.

www.ingramcontent.com/pod-product-compliance
Lightning Source LLC
Chambersburg PA
CBHW070054120526
44588CB00033B/1437